Learn Type-Driven Development

Benefit from type systems to build reliable and safe applications using ReasonML 3

Yawar Amin
Kamon Ayeva

BIRMINGHAM - MUMBAI

Learn Type-Driven Development

Commissioning Editor: Aaron Lazar
Acquisition Editor: Alok Dhuri
Content Development Editor: Anugraha Arunagiri
Technical Editor: Divya Vadhyar
Copy Editor: Safis Editing
Project Coordinator: Ulhas Kambali
Proofreader: Safis Editing
Indexer: Aishwarya Gangawane
Graphics: Tania Dutta
Production Coordinator: Arvindkumar Gupta

First published: December 2018

Production reference: 1241218

Published by Packt Publishing Ltd.
Livery Place
35 Livery Street
Birmingham
B3 2PB, UK.

ISBN 978-1-78883-801-6

www.packt.com

`mapt.io`

Mapt is an online digital library that gives you full access to over 5,000 books and videos, as well as industry leading tools, to help you plan your personal development and advance your career. For more information, please visit our website.

Why subscribe?

- Spend less time learning and more time coding with practical eBooks and videos from over 4,000 industry professionals

- Improve your learning with Skill Plans designed especially for you

- Get a free eBook or video every month

- Mapt is fully searchable

- Copy and paste, print, and bookmark content

Packt.com

Did you know that Packt offers eBook versions of every book published, with PDF and ePub files available? You can upgrade to the eBook version at `www.Packt.com` and, as a print book customer, you are entitled to a discount on the eBook copy. Get in touch with us at `customercare@packtpub.com` for more details.

At `www.Packt.com`, you can also read a collection of free technical articles, sign up for a range of free newsletters, and receive exclusive discounts and offers on Packt books and eBooks.

Contributors

About the authors

Yawar Amin is a software engineer working in Toronto, Canada. He has worked on data science-based recommendation systems, customer-facing applications, and large data engineering projects. In his spare time, he likes to read, write, and use the Oxford comma whenever he can.

I would like to thank those people whose efforts drive the ReasonML community forward. Beginning with those individuals who study and talk about type theory, to those who implemented the powerful and industrial-grade ML family languages, and, of course, the ReasonML project creators and community leaders who spend their days bringing this powerful language into the mainstream by engineering solid, reliable, and fun software.

This book would not have been possible either without my family. My parents ensured that I would be a lifelong reader; my brother makes sure I don't take myself too seriously; and my grandparents made sure I know that I have a history and a place I come from.

Kamon Ayeva is a web developer/DevOps engineer working with a variety of tools. He spends most of his time building projects using Python's powerful scripting capabilities, add-on libraries, and web frameworks such as Django or Flask. Kamon has been using Python in professional contexts for more than 12 years. Based on his recent experience of using the type system that was added to Python 3, as well as developing a user interface using the React framework, latterly, he has started exploring type-driven development in JavaScript.

About the reviewer

Hari Gopal is the engineering lead at SV.CO and has been a professional programmer since 2009. He has worked on a variety of products using a range of programming languages, including Ruby, JavaScript, Python, Java, PHP, and, most recently, ReasonML (OCaml). He is currently building an open source password management tool called Turaku.

Packt is searching for authors like you

If you're interested in becoming an author for Packt, please visit `authors.packtpub.com` and apply today. We have worked with thousands of developers and tech professionals, just like you, to help them share their insight with the global tech community. You can make a general application, apply for a specific hot topic that we are recruiting an author for, or submit your own idea.

Table of Contents

Preface

Type-driven development is an approach to programming that uses a static-type system to achieve desirable attributes, such as safety and efficiency. This book will cover type-driven development using the ReasonML language and explains how to put its type system to use in order to check that your code is logically consistent. We use types to express relationships and other assumptions directly in the code, and these assumptions are enforced by the ReasonML compiler before the code is run.

Who this book is for

If you've ever wrestled with this problem: *Undefined is not a function*, then this book might be for you. If you're looking for a way to write less defensive code, fewer trivial tests, and not worry about breaking code if you try to refactor, then you may be interested in the concepts of type-driven development.

This book is for you if you are a programmer (it doesn't matter what kind) who's interested in writing safe, efficient code. There are many techniques and processes for achieving that, of course, but type-driven development is one of the most mainstream and accessible.

That being said, this book presents type-driven development using a relatively unfamiliar language. I've tried to write as plainly as possible; but to follow along, you'll still need to learn the rules and logic of a powerful type system. You will reach a point where your mind works in tandem with the compiler, but that will take time and patience. The reward will be that the compiler becomes your friend in writing safer and more correct code.

If you're willing to go on this journey and learn the rules of the type system, then this book is for you.

What this book covers

Chapter 1, *Starting Type-Driven Development*, introduces type-driven development and its primary benefits. It gets you started with the ReasonML language and its tooling, it sets up a tutorial project that we will use throughout this book, and it shows where to go for further help and resources.

Chapter 2, *Programming with Types and Values,* sets up an edit-compile workflow for fast development, and introduces a number of foundational concepts, such as types and values. It also covers how a static typing compiler works and how it is different from dynamic typing.

Chapter 3, *Packaging Types and Values Together,* shows how to write modular code and take advantage of Reason's first-class module support to achieve abstraction, information hiding, and API documentation.

Chapter 4, *Grouping Values Together in Types,* covers types that may contain multiple values of different types at once, the various ways to construct these product types, and how best to use them.

Chapter 5, *Putting Alternative Values in Types,* covers types that may contain only one value at a time of possibly many different types. We cover how these sum types are different from product types, and how and when to use them.

Chapter 6, *Making Types that Can Slot into Any Other Type,* covers generics, type parameters, how to make sum and product types generic, and the restrictions of working with generics.

Chapter 7, *Making Types that Represent Operations,* covers functions and what their desirable properties are in type-driven development, how to create functions and how they work, and how to use them with achieve techniques such as dependency injection and inversion of control.

Chapter 8, *Reusing Code with Many Different Types,* covers parametric polymorphism, a powerful technique in type-driven development for writing code that can be extended and reused without the old and new code having to know about each other's implementation details.

Chapter 9, *Extending Types with New Behavior,* covers techniques that can be used to improve code reuse and extend parts of an implementation.

Chapter 10, *Bringing It All Together,* explains how to tie together many different techniques to explore an implementation when trying to solve a problem in a type-driven way.

To get the most out of this book

You should have experience with at least one programming language. It doesn't have to be JavaScript or ReasonML, even though we use these languages as examples of dynamic and statically-typed languages in this book.

You should have a macOS, Linux, or Windows computer on which to install ReasonML and the associated software.

You should type in and compile (in some cases, run) the examples shown throughout the chapters. The examples have been designed to show the ideas covered, and deliberately trying out some of the negative examples shown in the chapters will be very instructive.

Download the example code files

You can download the example code files for this book from your account at www.packt.com. If you purchased this book elsewhere, you can visit www.packt.com/support and register to have the files emailed directly to you.

You can download the code files by following these steps:

1. Log in or register at www.packt.com.
2. Select the **SUPPORT** tab.
3. Click on **Code Downloads & Errata**.
4. Enter the name of the book in the **Search** box and follow the onscreen instructions.

Once the file is downloaded, please make sure that you unzip or extract the folder using the latest version of:

- WinRAR/7-Zip for Windows
- Zipeg/iZip/UnRarX for Mac
- 7-Zip/PeaZip for Linux

The code bundle for the book is also hosted on GitHub at https://github.com/PacktPublishing/Learn-Type-Driven-Development. We also have other code bundles from our rich catalog of books and videos available at https://github.com/PacktPublishing/. Check them out!

Conventions used

There are a number of text conventions used throughout this book.

CodeInText: Indicates code words in text, database table names, folder names, filenames, file extensions, pathnames, dummy URLs, user input, and Twitter handles. Here is an example: "Mount the downloaded WebStorm-10*.dmg disk image file as another disk in your system".

A block of code is set as follows:

```
let sumOfSquares(x: int, y: int) = { /* (1) */
   let xSq = x * x;
   let ySq = y * y;
   xSq + ySq
};
```

The code is *highlighted* as follows:

- Types are **bolded**
- Values are *slanted*
- Language-reserved words (keywords) are <u>underlined</u>

Also note that numbered comments are added to certain points in the code that need further explanation, for example:

1. This note explains the code marked with the comment `/* (1) */`

Any command-line input or output is written as follows:

```
$ mkdir css
$ cd css
```

Bold: Indicates a new term, an important word, or words that you see on screen. For example, words in menus or dialog boxes appear in the text like this. Here is an example: "Select **System info** from the **Administration** panel".

Warnings or important notes appear like this.

Tips and tricks appear like this.

Get in touch

Feedback from our readers is always welcome.

General feedback: Email customercare@packtpub.com and mention the book title in the subject of your message. If you have questions about any aspect of this book, please email us at customercare@packtpub.com.

Errata: Although we have taken every care to ensure the accuracy of our content, mistakes do happen. If you have found a mistake in this book, we would be grateful if you would report this to us. Please visit www.packtpub.com/submit-errata, selecting your book, clicking on the Errata Submission Form link, and entering the details.

Piracy: If you come across any illegal copies of our works in any form on the internet, we would be grateful if you would provide us with the location address or website name. Please contact us at copyright@packt.com with a link to the material.

If you are interested in becoming an author: If there is a topic that you have expertise in, and you are interested in either writing or contributing to a book, please visit authors.packtpub.com.

Reviews

Please leave a review. Once you have read and used this book, why not leave a review on the site that you purchased it from? Potential readers can then see and use your unbiased opinion to make purchase decisions, we at Packt can understand what you think about our products, and our authors can see your feedback on their book. Thank you!

For more information about Packt, please visit packt.com.

1
Starting Type-Driven Development

In this book, we are exploring the techniques and idioms available in type-driven development. Some people also refer to type-driven development as type-level programming. Static types offer several benefits, including:

- Preventing incorrect code from getting a chance to run
- Documenting the current codebase
- Helping to correctly refactor the codebase by pointing out any parts of code you may have missed
- Offering richer IDE support, for example, auto-completion
- Better performance when the compiler knows types and can optimize code accordingly

Type-driven development is the practice of using static types to restrict what your code can do. Normally, your programming language gives you enough power to represent any computation. With type-driven development, you are essentially trying to make it impossible for your code to do undesirable things.

In this chapter, we will do some basic critical analysis of a piece of code and look at the possible errors it may contain. We'll also introduce ReasonML, the language we will use to learn type-driven development and compare it with JavaScript. We'll get started with a basic Reason project and then introduce Reason, as well as its related communities and ecosystems.

In this chapter, we will cover the following topics:

- The main idea and benefits of type-driven development
- Dynamically typed code versus its statically typed ReasonML equivalent
- The Reason language, ecosystem, and related projects
- How to set up a basic Reason project, which we will use throughout this book
- The Try Reason online playground

Analyzing code for hidden errors

Let's suppose that you have the following JavaScript:

```
// src/Ch01/Ch01_Demo.js
function makePerson(id, name) { return {id, name}; }
```

A lot of things can go wrong with the preceding code; they are as follows:

- The caller can pass in nulls or undefined values as arguments
- The caller can pass in unintended types of arguments
- The caller can manipulate the returned `person` object any way they like, for example, they can add or remove properties

In other words, this code doesn't prevent a number of potential errors. In JavaScript, we have linters, such as ESLint (`https://eslint.org/`), that check for a lot of possible errors, but you have to remember to find them, enable them, and then work around their limitations. A linter can be helpful in various other ways, such as by pointing out the recommended best practices in a coding style. However, linters in JavaScript are often re-purposed to perform static type checking tasks as well; because they offer so much flexibility and need to be configured (in fact, people usually upload their preferred sets of configuration for different styles of programming), there may be large differences in what exactly gets checked across different codebases.

Adding types

With a static type system, we can restrict our `makePerson` function in quite a few ways. Here's an example using ReasonML, the language that we're using in this book to learn type-driven development:

```
/* src/Ch01/Ch01_Demo.re */
type person = {id: int, name: string};
let makePerson(id, name) = {id, name};
```

Here, we define a new data type, `person`, and a function that creates a value of the type given the required arguments. We have one more line in the preceding code than we do in the JavaScript code, but in exchange, we get the following guarantees:

- The caller cannot pass in null or undefined arguments
- The caller cannot pass in the wrong types of arguments
- The caller cannot mutate the result value of the function

Notice in the previous example that we didn't have to declare the argument or types for the `makePerson` function. This is because ReasonML has great type inference that automatically understands that `int`, `string`, and `person` must be the only possible types allowed for those parts of the function.

ReasonML will compile the previous code into the following JavaScript:

```
// src/Ch01/Ch01_Demo.bs.js
function makePerson(id, name) { return [id, name]; }
```

As you can see, the preceding code looks almost exactly like the JavaScript we wrote earlier—the main difference is that Reason's JavaScript compiler turns records (which we'll explore later) into JavaScript arrays to take advantage of their speed.

This is just a glimpse of what static types can do to your codebase. In the coming chapters, we'll have a look at many more practical applications.

ReasonML

We're going to explore type-driven development using ReasonML (`https://reasonml.github.io/`). Reason is a JavaScript-like syntax and is also a set of tools for OCaml (`https://ocaml.org/`). OCaml is a mature statically typed functional programming language with excellent support for object-oriented and modular programming.

We're going to write Reason code and compile it to JavaScript using the BuckleScript compiler (https://bucklescript.github.io/). BuckleScript takes input from Reason code and outputs essentially a simple subset of ES5 (that is, no ES2015-style classes, no arrow functions, and so on). This will allow us to write strongly statically typed code and see what the output JavaScript looks like with all the types stripped away.

 BuckleScript, by default, outputs JavaScript files with the extension .bs.js to distinguish them from your other JS files. You can see this in the example output file, src/Ch01/Ch01_Demo.bs.js.

The Reason toolkit currently consists of:

- A code formatting and syntax translation tool, refmt
- An interactive code evaluation environment, rtop
- A build manager for native-compilation projects (we won't need this one for this book), rebuild
- A tool that provides intellisense abilities to editors, ocamlmerlin-reason

These tools work together to provide a minimal, yet powerful, development experience. Together with a good editor (we recommend Visual Studio Code), they cover most of your day-to-day development needs.

Why ReasonML?

So why have we chosen ReasonML over something else? For example, TypeScript and Flow are popular languages that target JavaScript today (among many others), but we chose Reason because:

- It has a powerful and elegant type system, which neatly fits together many type-driven development concepts
- Its JavaScript compiler (BuckleScript) has incredibly fast compiles, optimization, and high-quality dead-code elimination; fast compiles are great to have if you're doing type-driven development, and performant code is great to have in any system
- It has a very helpful and enthusiastic community that's very accessible
- It gives you access to the mature OCaml community and its aggregated knowledge base

We will take advantage of the contrasts between the two languages to understand how statically typed Reason code is converted into dynamically typed JavaScript code yet still runs safely by design.

Getting started with ReasonML

The Reason website has a great quickstart guide as well as tutorials for setting up editor support. First, install NodeJS to get the **node package manager** (**npm**). Then, run the following:

```
npm install -g bs-platform
cd <your-projects-folder>
bsb -init learning-tydd-reason -theme basic-reason
cd learning-tydd-reason
```

Now we can do an initial compile with the following command:

```
bsb -make-world
```

The preceding command builds your entire project and its dependencies recursively. It will be almost instantaneous.

It's worth mentioning that we actually recommend running the preceding shell commands (substituting in your actual projects folder, of course), because throughout this book, we're going to arrange the code examples in the form of a single project, `learning-tydd-reason`, and the code examples that you type into the various given file names will fit together to make up that project.

You will almost certainly want to set up editor support in Reason so that you can get things like autocompletion and go to definition. The guides available on the ReasonML website (`https://reasonml.github.io/docs/en/global-installation.html`) are very helpful for this. Currently, Visual Studio Code (`http://code.visualstudio.com/`) is the best-supported editor; you will probably get the best results from using that.

If you are trying to decide on the install method, we would personally recommend the OPAM method (**OPAM** is the abbreviation of **OCaml Package Manager**).

Using Try Reason

Reason provides a fantastic resource for learners: an online Reason-to-JavaScript compiler and evaluator. To access it, go to the Reason website and click **Try** in the navigation bar at the top. You can use it to quickly try out different ideas.

Let's run through a quick example using Try Reason to get our bearings. Type in the example code from `src/Ch01/Ch01_Demo.re` into the **Reason** section of the Try Reason web app. Now add the following line after that:

```
let bob = makePerson(1, "Bob");
```

Now if you examine the output JS, you should see that the following changes have been made:

- Types have been stripped away
- Records have been transformed into arrays without field names (records are roughly like C structs or JavaScript objects)
- Every declared value is explicitly exported (made public)

Note that we have purposely introduced very little actual Reason syntax in this chapter. If you are curious to explore the syntax (which is very similar to JavaScript at its core), it's best if you explore the excellent Reason website documentation. Since the focus of this book is type-driven development, in the upcoming chapters we will introduce all the syntax we will need and discuss its impact on our understanding of the code.

Going further

The ReasonML community is a helpful, fast-growing one. If you need help with anything, don't be afraid to ask. You'll only be a beginner once, and once you're comfortable, you'll be able to help other beginners. Check out the community page at `https://reasonml.github.io/docs/en/community.html` and drop by the discord chat as the first point of contact.

Summary

In this chapter, we introduced the basic ideas of type-driven development and critically analyzed a piece of dynamically-typed code to explore its potential error conditions that would be prevented by adding static types. We also introduced the ReasonML language and its ecosystem, set up our own Reason project, and got a glimpse of how it can compile statically typed code to JavaScript.

The next chapter will be an important one—we'll delve more into types, values, and working in Reason. See you there!

Programming with Types and Values

2

In the previous chapter, we looked at type-driven development using ReasonML, but what are types exactly? And how do they interact with other parts of your program? How do they help you on a regular basis, and what does it look like to use a strong static type system with type inference?

In this chapter, we will cover the following topics:

- Setting up an editor workflow
- Types and values
- Immutable values and memory
- Static versus dynamic typing
- Type erasure
- Syntax errors
- Type errors and inference
- Unification

Workflow

To get the most from this chapter, we will set up a comfortable edit-compile workflow. We recommend placing two windows side-by-side in your editor. VSCode supports this functionality with the **View** | **Split Editor** command. On one side, load a Reason source file; on the other side, load the JavaScript output file (once it is initially compiled). Then in a terminal, run the following command:

```
bsb -w
```

The preceding command starts a build in *watch mode,* which automatically recompiles any parts of a project that are affected whenever you change any source code. In fact, watch mode is smart enough to also remove an outdated JavaScript output file whenever its corresponding Reason source file is deleted. The editor will also auto-reload the compiled JavaScript file whenever you save a Reason source file.

In VSCode, you can also open a terminal session directly below the files using the **View |
Integrated Terminal** command and run `bsb -w` to get a single integrated view of your entire workflow. This way, when there are compile errors, you won't have to switch windows to see them. Of course, you may prefer to work with two monitors and keep the terminal and compiler running on another screen so you don't have to switch windows—that's feasible, too.

Types and values

Let's set the stage for the rest of the book with a discussion of types and values. At its core, a type is a set of values. Think of the type `bool`, which is what Reason calls the normal Boolean type. A `bool` value can be one of two different things: `true` or `false`. We say that these values *inhabit* (live in) the type. Anything else is an error.

This raises an interesting question: *what does it mean to say? Anything else is an error' in this context? In fact, why should we care about types at all?*

To answer these questions, let's think about what should happen if we try to do the operation `"Bob" / 5`. What does it mean to divide the string `Bob` by the number 5?

If you can't think of a good answer, well neither can anyone else. It's kind of a meaningless question. It's like asking, *how does the color green taste?* (Although this may be a meaningful question for synesthetic people.)

Anyway, this is the simplest answer to why we care about types – to avoid having to deal with meaningless questions. To rule out meaningless operations, we simply make them type errors in the programs that execute the code. In other words, we get our compilers and interpreters to slot all our values into distinct types, or errors if any operations can't be meaningfully performed for the given types of values.

Static types

There are two possible times when type errors can happen: at compile time and at runtime. This is the crucial difference between static and dynamic type systems: static type systems are so called because they *statically analyze* programs and try to find type errors, while dynamic type systems are so called because they throw type errors dynamically, while they run the program.

 A dynamic type system will definitely find all the type errors in your program, provided it actually runs all the execution paths in it. Any paths that remain unexecuted may contain hidden type errors.

A static type system will try to find as many errors as possible without running your program. Normally, this is not a guarantee that you will catch all type errors before runtime. Some errors may slip through the **typechecker** and still hit you at runtime. Plus, a type system may make it difficult to express a program that you know is correct because it thinks it's not. You will want to pay close attention when this happens, though, as either the typechecker is correct, or your design will benefit from expressing the program in a different, accepted, way.

What do you gain?

With regard to the caveats mentioned earlier, what do static type systems actually give you?

- A good type system catches almost all type errors for you before runtime
- It accepts all or almost all programs that do not contain type errors

Being able to catch type errors before runtime is a very nice ability to have. It will help you to avoid possible downtime, expenses, lost business, and so on. Note that we mentioned a *good* type system. We should try to aim for the best type system we can get at our disposal. Since, Reason is OCaml, it automatically gets OCaml's powerful, safe, and expressive type system.

Static and dynamic environments

Let's develop a mental model for what happens in a program with types and values. At its core, a program is made up of a series of type and value definitions. For example:

```
/* src/Ch02/Ch02_Demo.re */
type person = {id: int, name: string};
type company = {id: int, name: string, employees: list(person)};

let bob = {id: 1, name: "Bob"};
let acmeCo = {id: 1, name: "Acme Co.", employees: [bob]};
```

Here, we're defining `person` and `company` types, and then allocating a person (`bob`) and a company he works for (`acmeCo`).

Without worrying too much about the syntax (we will introduce this in `Chapter 4`, *Group Values Together in Types*), let's think about how the programming environment sees this program.

In a statically typed programming language, the typechecker and runtime environment together make up the *static* and *dynamic environments*. These are areas where type definitions are stored while typechecking takes place, and where value definitions are stored during program execution (runtime). We can think of these as two distinct areas that are only relevant during the distinct phases of compilation and runtime. After compilation, all type information is wiped out (*type erasure*), but during runtime the dynamic environment becomes active in memory (that is, the stack and the heap).

Here is how the static and dynamic environments look for the preceding code:

Static Environment	Dynamic Environment
`type person;`	
`type company;` (refers to `person`)	
	`let bob;`
	`let acmeCo;` (refers to `bob`)

Example of static and dynamic environments (evaluated top to bottom)

In each of the static and dynamic environments, each definition is allowed to refer to definitions that came before it. This is a crucial abstraction technique – it's how we build larger programs out of smaller ones at both the type and value levels.

TIP

There are no references between the static and dynamic environments – values don't exist at compile time and types don't exist at runtime. This may come a surprise as we do mix them in one place: the source code.

Among other things, this strict separation balances the needs of safety and efficiency. Note that this is in sharp contrast to dynamic typing, where types exist at runtime as well, and must be checked before every operation.

Values

It's important to understand how values work in Reason. We've seen that they come into play at runtime and live in memory but it's also important to know that, by default, all values are immutable –effectively, constants. There are a couple of exceptions, which we will cover, but generally we will work in a style where we don't try to change values, and instead just create new values out of old ones. This is a style that is well-supported by Reason and is a foundation of functional programming.

There is a syntax for binding values to names, which is as follows:

```
let PATTERN = VALUE;
```

The preceding syntax slots the value on the right-hand side into the shape described in the left-hand side, as long as their shapes match. The general name for this concept is *pattern matching*, and we will see it a lot in this book.

So far, the patterns (to the left of =) we've seen have been just simple names, such as:

```
let x = 1;
```

The preceding pattern has allowed us to capture the entire value in the name and reuse it later. The way it works is that Reason checks that the value (1) can fit inside the pattern (x). In this simple case, there is nothing about the pattern that prevents the value from fitting inside. We call this an *irrefutable pattern*. In further chapters, we will see examples of *refutable* patterns and how they behave.

Wherever you see the keyword `let`, you should understand that it may be allocating memory, if:

- The bound value is a literal (for example, `"Bob"`), or
- The bound value is the result of a function or operator call, and the function or operator call allocates a new value in memory

The other cases are mainly of bindings to existing values or bindings to function calls that don't allocate.

In this book, we won't be worrying too much about allocation and memory use, but we will look at a couple of techniques of how to reduce them when necessary, which can come in handy when trying to boost performance.

Scoping and shadowing

Whenever we define values, they exist (in the dynamic environment) in a scope, in which all previously defined names are available but only until the end of the scope. Scopes are nested inside each other, starting with the *top level* scope (the definitions at the file level), and nested scopes inside braces ({ . . . }). For example:

```
/* src/Ch02/Ch02_Scope.re */
let x = 1;

let y = x + 1;

let z = {
  let result = 0;
  result + x + y
};
```

Here, x and y are in the top level scope, where y can access x by name because x is defined before y; z can access both for the same reason. However, note the definition of `result` in the nested scope introduced by the braces. The name `result` is only available from the point it is defined up until the closing brace; outside of that scope, referring to `result` will result in a compile error (specifically, a *name error,* which we will talk about later in the chapter).

Because Reason puts all definitions in certain scopes, we can define the same name more than once in the same scope or in a nested scope. This is called **shadowing** because the new definition hides the old one until the new one goes out of scope. Of course, if the old and new names go out of scope together (that is, they're in the same scope), the old name is effectively hidden forever. The following codeblock is an example of this:

```
/* src/Ch02/Ch02_Shadowing.re */
let name = "Bob";
let age = "33";

let greeting = {
  let age = "34";
  "Hello, " ++ name ++ " aged " ++ age;
```

```
};

let name = "Jim";
let greeting2 = "Hello, " ++ name ++ " aged " ++ age;
```

Let's now take a look at the output JavaScript as follows:

```
// src/Ch02/Ch02_Shadowing.bs.js
var age = "33";
var greeting = "Hello, Bob aged 34";
var name = "Jim";
var greeting2 = "Hello, Jim aged 33";
```

Notice how Bob's age is 34 in his `greeting` – the `age` in the `greeting` scope shadows `age` in the top level scope. However, as soon as that scope ends (with the closing brace), the original `age` becomes visible again and is used in Jim's `greeting2`.

However, the second `name` binding (`"Jim"`) permanently shadows the first one because they are both in the top level scope. In fact, since the first `name` and the inner `age` will never be visible again, the BuckleScript compiler doesn't even bother to output them, instead directly inlining their values.

Understanding type erasure

To concretely grasp the effect of static/dynamic separation, let's look at type erasure, which is something that happens when we compile the preceding code to JavaScript. The following is the output with all redundant comments removed:

```
// src/Ch02/Ch02_Demo.bs.js
var bob = [1, "Bob"];
var acmeCo_002 = [bob, 0];
var acmeCo = [1, "Acme Co.", acmeCo_002];
```

As we mentioned earlier, BuckleScript compiles Reason record types into JavaScript arrays with the corresponding number of elements. BuckleScript, in fact, performs quite a number of optimizations for you. Some of these come from its underlying OCaml compiler technology, which has been developed since the 1990s, but other things are quite unique in the world of language-to-JavaScript compilers.

Notice that BuckleScript has wiped out both the type definitions and has output only the minimum number of values it actually needs for runtime. The important thing to understand here is that all the output values follow the laws introduced by their corresponding types; for example, the `Bob` value, of type `person`, can only be an array with two elements (a number and a string, corresponding to the two fields in the person record), and the `acmeCo` value can only be an array with three elements of the correct types. Anything else is impossible – with a mathematical degree of certainty – even in output JavaScript code, because code that doesn't pass the typing rules (that is, doesn't typecheck) would not even compile.

Errors

We mentioned earlier that the compiler will raise errors if it cannot make sense of a piece of code it comes across. There are a few different kinds of compiler errors, and they are as follows

- Syntax errors
- Type errors
- Name errors
- Stale interface errors (which we'll cover in the next chapter)
- Compiler bugs (these are rare but shouldn't be discounted)

The two most common types of error that we will deal with are syntax errors and type errors. Name errors are fairly simple to avoid: always start type names with a lowercase letter and ensure that the names you refer to in your code were defined before you refer to them. (Reason supports *cyclic references* but not *forward references*; we'll cover cyclic references later on.)

Syntax errors

Syntax errors are a basic kind of error and happen when the compiler literally can't make sense of the source code, for example:

```
type person = {id: int; name: string};
```

Can you spot the error in the preceding code? If you compare it with the `person` definition in `src/Ch02/Ch02_Demo.re`, you should be able to. In any case, the compiler will tell you (usually fairly accurately) where to look. The only problem is you'll have to learn to sift through the compiler output to find the exact error, as follows:

```
(Output from bsb -w)
>>>> Start compiling
Rebuilding since [ [ 'change', 'Ch02_Demo.re' ] ]
ninja: Entering directory `lib/bs'
[1/2] Building src/Ch02/Ch02_Demo.mlast
FAILED: src/Ch02/Ch02_Demo.mlast
/usr/local/lib/node_modules/bs-platform/lib/bsc.exe -pp
"/usr/local/lib/node_modules/bs-platform/lib/refmt3.exe -print binary"    -
w -30-40+6+7+27+32..39+44+45+101 -warn-error +3 -bs-suffix -nostdlib -I
'/Users/yawar/src/learning-tydd-reason/node_modules/bs-platform/lib/ocaml'
-no-alias-deps -color always -c -o src/Ch02/Ch02_Demo.mlast -bs-syntax-only
-bs-binary-ast -impl /Users/yawar/src/learning-tydd-
reason/src/Ch02/Ch02_Demo.re
File "/Users/yawar/src/learning-tydd-reason/src/Ch02/Ch02_Demo.re", line 2,
characters 23-24:
Error: 438: <UNKNOWN SYNTAX ERROR>
File "/Users/yawar/src/learning-tydd-reason/src/Ch02/Ch02_Demo.re", line 1,
characters 0-0:
Error: Error while running external preprocessor
Command line: /usr/local/lib/node_modules/bs-platform/lib/refmt3.exe -print
binary '/Users/yawar/src/learning-tydd-reason/src/Ch02/Ch02_Demo.re' >
/var/folders/xg/6jbw_1bj5h35b4lt7rygs12w0000gn/T/ocamlppf72c18

ninja: error: rebuilding 'build.ninja': subcommand failed
>>>> Finish compiling(exit: 1)
```

Syntax errors start with the text `File "/path/to/file", line L, characters C1-C2:` (where L, C1, and C2 are the actual line and character numbers). The error message, `<UNKNOWN SYNTAX ERROR>`, is not too helpful, but the line and character positions pinpoint the location pretty well. Confusingly, there is also another error message starting in the same way, but this time with `line 1` and `characters 0-0: Error while running external preprocessor`. This is Reason's way of redundantly saying it couldn't understand the code, and is hopefully going away soon!

In our example, the error points at the 23rd and 24th characters, where you see a semicolon and space; if you compare that with the correct version of the code, you see that it should be a comma and space.

When you're starting out with Reason, you should expect to see more of these syntax errors, and to spend some time working through exactly why they're happening. As you learn the syntax, you can expect to be able to tell just by looking at it that a piece of code doesn't contain the correct syntax. The correct syntax is available in Reason's excellent reference documentation.

Type errors and inference

The other main kind of compiler error you will see is a **type error**. A type error is an error that arises when a type (or a value of a type) is used in a way that's not allowed by the type definition.

These are more interesting errors because you're likely to come across them for the rest of your programming career, during which you should expect to continue seeing large productivity and code quality benefits from type errors forcing better design thinking and bug reduction.

Type errors are also heavily tied into Reason's type inference engine, which through a process of elimination works out exactly what the types should be for every piece of the code. Let's look at a few simple type errors and the code that will trigger them. We will also explain the type inference rules that led to the error.

First, let's try the division problem we posted earlier (the bold parts are colored red in Reason's error message):

```
(Output from bsb -w)
  We've found a bug for you!
  /Users/yawar/src/learning-tydd-reason/src/Ch02/Ch02_Demo.re 8:14-18

  6 | /* ... elided ... */
  7 |
  8 | let result = "Bob" / 5;

  This has type:
    string
  But somewhere wanted:
    int
```

Let's look at the process of elimination by which Reason arrives at type errors:

- Assigns types to the smallest possible parts of the expression, one by one
- Tries to fit all the types together like puzzle pieces
  - If they fit, pass typechecker
  - If they don't fit, raise a type error

The following diagram shows the type inference and checking process (read from left to right):

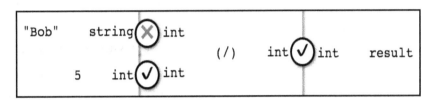

The type error arises from the fact that `"Bob"` is a string (anything inside double-quotes is inferred to be a string), whereas the division operator (`/`) by definition requires two `int` variables as input. However, Reason can still infer `result` to be an `int` because it knows the division operator outputs an `int`.

Now, let's try a slightly more interesting type error, from not creating a record correctly, shown as follows:

```
(Output from bsb -w)
We've found a bug for you!
/Users/yawar/src/learning-tydd-reason/src/Ch02/Ch02_Demo.re 6:51-53

4 |
5 |   let bob = {id: 1, name: "Bob"};
6 |   let acmeCo = {id: 1, name: "Acme Co.", employees: bob};

  This has type:
person
But somewhere wanted:
list (person)
```

The following diagram shows the typechecking process for a record:

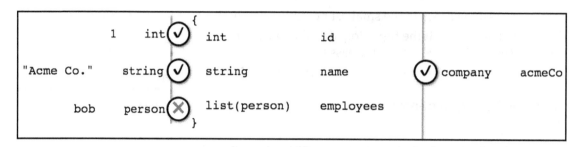

Here, the type error arises because one of the components of the record does not have the correct type. You can compare the code in the error message with the source code to exact

You may be curious to know why the division type error was reported the way it was, when it may have been more natural to work from left to right and produce an error like **string does not support division by ints**. This is because the typechecker works on the *abstract syntax tree* of the program – that is, an internal representation of the program itself after it has been parsed (and verified as free of syntax errors). The AST is structured, as you might have guessed, as a tree, and in the tree, operations and function calls are the parent nodes of their arguments. So, the operations are assigned types first and then their arguments. Hence you see "Bob" as the thing that caused the type mismatch, instead of (/).

Theoretically, though, typechecking could go in either direction – from the root of the AST to its leaf nodes or the other way round as normal. You may often hear the process of fitting the types together referred to as **unification**, which means the same thing. If instead of "Bob", the first operand had been, for example, 10 (of type int), Reason would have been able to unify their types (int and int) and thus pass typechecking.

Summary

In this chapter, we covered a lot of ground, including setting up an editorial workflow, learning about types and values, static and dynamic typing, Reason's separation between compile time and runtime and its type erasure, syntax, and type errors, as well as inference and unification.

In future chapters, we will build on this chapter and introduce many more static typing techniques and the potential type errors that we may see from using them.

3
Packaging Types and Values Together

ReasonML has fantastic support for the software engineering practice of dividing programs into small, modular components that can be swapped out for each other.

In this chapter, we will cover:

- Modules and how they can be used to package types and values together
- The difference between file modules and syntactic modules
- Module signatures (both file and syntactic)
- Using signatures to achieve information hiding
- Using signatures to achieve type abstraction
- Achieving zero-cost abstraction

Modules are groups of types and values accessible under a single name. This can be incredibly useful when you want to associate some types and operations together to make them easier to find and use together. They are kind of like **namespaces** in other languages, but more powerful because they can be composed in various ways.

Let's look at how to make some modules.

File modules

It turns out we've already made some modules! Reason treats the `.re` source files as modules, so our `src/Ch01/Ch01_Demo.re` and `src/Ch02/Ch02_Demo.re` files are automatically available as modules, with the names `Ch01_Demo` and `Ch02_Demo`, respectively. In the Reason world, these are called **implementation files**. We will informally refer to them as **file modules**.

Reason names file modules purely from their file names, ignoring their directory nesting. It makes every module automatically available from every other module, regardless of where they are physically in the project. This is why we were careful to name our modules with chapter prefixes; otherwise, files from different chapters but with the same names would confuse the compiler.

Let's take advantage of Reason's automatic module resolution, by creating a new (file) module that refers to something in an existing module:

```
/* src/Ch03/Ch03_Greet.re */
let greet(person: Ch02_Demo.person) = /* (1), (2), (3) */
  "Hello, " ++ /* (4), (5) */
  person.name ++
  " with ID " ++
  string_of_int(person.id) ++ /* (6) */
  "!";
```

Here we're defining a function that knows how to greet people with a name and an ID. There are a few things happening in this example (marked by the numbered comments):

1. We assign a type to the `person` function parameter by appending a colon followed by the type. You can read this as "*person has type c h 0 2 demo dot person*". We can assign types to any function parameters in Reason; they are almost always optional though, because of type inference. In this case, we wanted to be explicit because of a subtle issue: there are actually two different record types (`person` and `company`) with the `name` and `id` fields in the `Ch02_Demo` module, and we need to distinguish between them.

2. Function definitions have a body consisting of a single expression; this can also be a compound expression delimited by brackets (we'll see examples later).

3. We can have a `person` value and a `person` type–they don't clash because Reason stores them separately, in the static and dynamic environments.

4. Reason is whitespace-insensitive; you can lay out your code any way you want, as long as you separate bindings with a semicolon. For most codebases, you would actually just use the Reason formatter tool, `refmt`, which would automatically take care of all formatting.

5. The ++ operator in Reason concatenates two strings (and nothing else!) together.

6. `person.id` is an `int`, so we can't concatenate it with its surrounding strings–unless we convert it to a string with the built-in `string_of_int` function. Reason has strict, strong typing, and doesn't implicitly convert between types (not even between `int` and `float` variables).

To understand what Reason is doing for us, let's look at the relevant part of the output JavaScript:

```
// src/Ch03/Ch03_Greet.bs.js
function greet(person) {
  return "Hello, "
    + person[1]
    + " with ID "
    + String(person[0])
    + "!";
}
```

 I've cleaned and rearranged the JavaScript output somewhat, without changing its meaning.

As usual, we see the types are completely erased, and the output is concerned only with values. Based on the types, though, the Reason compiler knew to access the person's name at array index 1 and ID at index 0. Also, it knows to ensure that `person[0]` gets converted into a string by using the JavaScript string constructor.

In the JavaScript world, we'd say that such a conversion is unnecessary. But in the statically typed Reason world, the compiler keeps a tally of the types of all values and ensures they interact only according to the rules of their types. Thus we ensure that a number can't accidentally be added to a series of strings.

On a larger scale, notice that the fact that Reason files are modules is not directly visible in the JavaScript output code–except that the Reason files are directly compiled, with a one-to-one relationship, to JavaScript modules.

Syntactic modules

Let's look at another way of creating modules in Reason: **syntactic modules**. These are modules that are defined using Reason's module syntax. Here's an example:

```
/* src/Ch03/Ch03_Domain.re */
module Person = {
  type t = {id: int, name: string};
  let make(id, name) = {id, name};
};

module Company = {
  type t = {id: int, name: string, employees: list(Person.t)};
```

```
};
```

Here we define a `Domain` file module to contain two *nested* modules: `Person` and `Company`. These nested modules actually contain types similar to the ones we defined in `src/Ch02/Ch02_Demo.re`, but this time with both types named `t`.

 Let's digress a little into the type name `t`. This is a standard naming convention in the Reason ecosystem to mean the main type in the module. Usually, you refer to a module along with its main type, for example, `Person.t` or `Company.t`, so it's quite clear exactly which type you mean.

Syntactic modules have the following form: `module Name = {...bindings...};` and all the bindings are then available to outside consumers under the module name, for example, `Name.binding1`, and so on.

Earlier, we said that modules package types and values together. But in the preceding example, you can see that the `Ch03_Domain` file module itself contains two modules, `Person` and `Company`. I actually oversimplified before. Modules can recursively contain other modules! This is a great code organization and namespacing strategy.

Let's look at the (relevant part of the) JavaScript output to understand what the runtime effect of this domain module is:

```
// src/Ch03/Ch03_Domain.bs.js
function make(id, name) { return [id, name]; }

var Person = [make];
var Company = [];
exports.Person = Person;
exports.Company = Company;
```

The `Person` and `Company` modules are represented as JavaScript arrays, and their `t` types are completely erased, leaving the arrays almost empty. The arrays contain only what file-level module JavaScript output would contain: values. In fact, this is almost exactly how Reason represents modules when compiled to bytecode or native binary form.

 It is not, however, how you might expect a *nested module* to look in idiomatic JavaScript. Indeed, the BuckleScript compiler does not always emit completely idiomatic JavaScript output. Some of those cases can be fixed (indeed, some have already been); others are compromises that the compiler needs to make to efficiently convert Reason code into JavaScript.

Using a syntactic module

As you can see, modules are very cheap. They have almost no runtime effect. Let's look at the payoff of arranging our types into their own nested modules. We're going to try greeting a person again:

```
/* src/Ch03/Ch03_GreetAgain.re */
let greetAgain(person) = /* (1) */
  "Hello again, " ++
  person.Ch03_Domain.Person.name ++ /* (2) */
  " with ID " ++
  string_of_int(person.id) ++
  "!";
```

What's different from `src/Ch03/Ch03_Greet.re`?

1. We don't need to explicitly annotate the type of `person`
2. We need to tell Reason which module the `name` field is coming from, because, in order to prevent name clashes between record types that have the same field names, Reason doesn't automatically open up modules to look for type details

You might ask, is this really a payoff? We've just traded one kind of annotation (the explicit type signature) for another (the field name module prefix). While that is true, it's idiomatic for implementation code to have as few type annotations as possible and let the compiler infer as much as possible.

Type annotations do serve another purpose though, which is to document the types. In Reason, we have an explicit place to put type annotations that document our module types and serve some other useful purposes.

Module signatures

Module signatures, also known as **interfaces**, are an explicit place to put type annotations. But they actually serve several purposes:

- Export a module's public API
- Document the types of a module's public API
- Provide a place to put module documentation
- Hide non-public elements of a module
- Hide implementation details of types

Keeping in mind the points mentioned earlier, when would you *not* want to use a signature for your module? It's not set in stone, but my rule of thumb is to not use a signature when my API is experimental and still evolving (in semantic versioning terms, less than version 1.0.0.), or when the module is purely an application module and is not meant to be published as a library for others to consume (although the line between these is somewhat grainy).

Signatures come in two forms–**interface files** and **syntactic signatures**, corresponding to implementations. Interface files are Reason source files that contain signatures and nothing else. Syntactic signatures are signatures that are defined specifically using Reason's syntax support for signatures.

We will explore the previously mentioned points chiefly by using interface files, but also show examples of syntactic signatures as appropriate.

Exporting and documenting the public API

Let's look at an example of exporting and documenting a module's public API. This is an interface file:

```
/** src/Ch03/Ch03_GreetAgain.rei (1), (2)
    Contains a way to greet a person. */

/** Greet someone with a name and ID, again. (3) */
let greetAgain: Ch03_Domain.Person.t => string; /* (4) */
```

There are a few interesting things going on here:

1. Interface files must have the `.rei` (Reason Interface) file extension, with file names corresponding to the implementation file name.

2. We are using a new kind of comment, called a **documentation comment (doc comment)**, to write documentation that will be publicly exported along with the API. Doc comments start with `/**` and end with `*/`. There are tools in the Reason ecosystem that can understand doc comments and format them for readers. Note that we usually don't use doc comments in implementation (`.re`) files because it usually doesn't make sense to expose implementation-specific documentation to users.

3. Any item in a module can be documented with doc comments.

4. We use a value declaration to tell Reason to export a value from the module, with the given type. In this case, the type of the value is a function type–this one reads "*ch 0 3 domain person t arrow string*" meaning *take a chapter 3 domain person type as input and return a string as output.* We will cover functions in more detail in a future chapter.

So, what does this interface file compile to? As it turns out: nothing. Interface files are purely compile-time constructs; they don't exist at all at runtime. In fact, they are erased just like types because they are types. *Module interfaces are types.* A .rei file you write as an interface actually specifies the type of its corresponding .re implementation file.

Syntactic module signatures

Module signatures are also known as **module types**. Just like other types, module types specify what you can and can't do with values of their type; in other words, they specify the surface area of a module.

Here's an example of a syntactic module type and its usage:

```
/* src/Ch03/Ch03_ModuleType.re */
module type PersonType = {
  type t = {id: int, name: string};
  let make: (int, string) => t; /* (1) */
};

module Person: PersonType = { /* (2) */
  type t = {id: int, name: string};

  let massage(name) = String.trim(String.capitalize(name)); /* (3) */
  let make(id, name) = {id, name: massage(name)}; /* (4) */
};
```

A syntactic module type has the `module type Type = {...declarations...};` form and specifies exactly what will be exported from a module that conforms to the type. Some key points to note in the previous example:

1. We declare a function's (make) type with the `let funName: (param1Type, ..., paramNType) => returnType;` syntax.

2. We declare that a module conforms to a module type by appending a colon followed by the module type.

3. We define a `massage` function to properly case and trim input names, but this function is not declared in the module type, so it's never exported (that is, users of this module won't be able to access `massage`).

4. We give a record field a specific expression as its value by using the `name: expression` syntax. We'll cover record type syntax more fully in a later chapter.

Let's take a look at the (relevant part of the) JavaScript output:

```
// src/Ch03/Ch03_ModuleType.bs.js
var $$String = require("bs-platform/lib/js/string.js"); // (1)
function make(id, name) {
  return [id, $$String.trim($$String.capitalize(name))]; // (2)
}
var Person = [make];
exports.Person = Person;
```

1. The Reason `String` module name is **damaged slightly** (with a `$$` prefix) in the output to avoid a name clash with the existing JavaScript `String` constructor.

2. The returned person array value doesn't call the `massage` function. In fact, BuckleScript doesn't even emit a `massage` function, having determined that it can be inlined.

Module errors

The fact that modules have types naturally leads to the fact that they can also throw type errors. Let's look at a couple of possible type errors related to modules.

Signature mismatch

What happens when we try to assign a module signature to a module that doesn't implement that interface properly? Check out the following:

```
(Output from bsb -w)
  We've found a bug for you!
  /Users/yawar/src/learning-tydd-reason/src/Ch03/Ch03_ModuleType.re
8:29-11:1
   6 | };
   7 |
   8 | module Person: PersonType = {
   9 |   type t = {id: int, name: string};
  10 |   let massage(name) = String.trim(String.capitalize(name));
  11 | };
```

```
   Signature mismatch:
   Modules do not match:
     { type t = { id: int, name: string, }; let massage: (string) => string;
}
   is not included in
     PersonType
   The value `make' is required but not provided
   File "/Users/yawar/src/learning-tydd-reason/src/Ch03/Ch03_ModuleType.re",
line 5, characters 3-31:
     Expected declaration
```

This message means that we forgot to include the `make` function in our implementation. The message is slightly strange, but makes sense if you know how Reason typechecks modules:

- It infers what it thinks should be the module type by examining the structure of the actual module
- It compares the inferred type to the annotated module type, `PersonType`
- It does not care about items that appear in the actual module but aren't declared in `PersonType` (it just hides those from the outside world)
- It does show errors on items that are declared in `PersonType` but are missing from the actual module

In short, you can't overpromise and under-deliver. Knowing this, you can interpret the error message: the inferred module type is on top, and the annotated module type is beneath, as shown in the following screenshot:

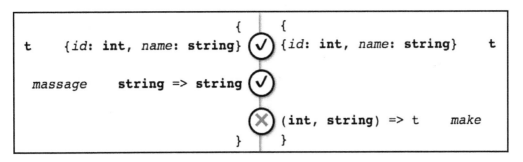

Module type mismatch error diagram

In Reason, modules are *structurally typed*: their types are made up of their structure, that is, by combining the types of their contained bindings in a syntactic form similar to the modules themselves. That's why we're able to write `module type Foo = {...declarations...};`—the `{...declarations...}` structural type is a first-class type by itself; we are just binding it to a name. A concrete result of this is that you can define a module and annotate it with a type directly, for example, `module Foo: {...declarations...} = {...bindings...};`. In a later chapter, we will examine structural typing further.

An important thing to understand is that you can't get a signature mismatch by implementing types and values in a different order from that in their signatures. You are still restricted to declaring or defining things before you use them, but the compiler will understand that a module conforms to a signature even if their declarations and definitions don't match up in exact order. To see a small example of this, look at the code sample in the upcoming *Type abstraction* section. The ordering of the `getter` functions is slightly different between the interface and the implementation.

This ordering flexibility can be a benefit if you're trying to arrange a module signature in a way that's easy to understand, that is, one that presents the most important items first. Sometimes, you don't need that level of flexibility, but you can always take advantage of it later if you find you do.

Value can't be found

What happens when we try to use something that doesn't exist in a module? Check out the following:

```
(Output from bsb -w)
  We've found a bug for you!
  /Users/yawar/src/learning-tydd-reason/src/Ch03/Ch03_ModuleType.re
10:23-40
   8 |    type t = {id: int, name: string};
   9 |
  10 |    let massage(name) = Ch03_Greet.process(name);
  11 |    let make(id, name) = {id, name: massage(name)};
  12 | };
  The value process can't be found in Ch03_Greet
```

Reason checks, at compile time, whether the type of the module (Ch03_Greet) exports the named value (process), and it fails the build otherwise. There is no way to use a value that does not exist.

Type abstraction

In Reason, you can hide the implementation of a type and reveal exactly what you choose to. This *type abstraction* is one of the best techniques for *preserving invariants* (rules that should be obeyed) in your codebase. Type abstraction also allows modules to be decoupled from each other's implementation details, and work only with the information they have from exported interfaces.

For example, look at the Ch03_ModuleType.Person module. It exports a t type to represent information about a person, and a make function to properly create values of the t type. The make function ensures that we properly trim and capitalize the names that we're given. We want to enforce the rule that names should have the proper casing and should not have surrounding whitespace.

The problem is we can do something like this:

```
let bob = {Ch03_ModuleType.Person.id: 1, name: " bob     "};
```

Because the Ch03.ModuleType.Person.t definition is exported, we can bypass the make function and directly create t values, breaking the rules that we want to apply for names.

We can solve this problem by making t an abstract type (note that we must define both the interface and implementation files, as shown ahead):

```
/** src/Ch03/Ch03_AbstractPerson.rei */

type id = int;
type name = string;
type t; /* (1) */

let make: (id, name) => t;
let id: t => id;
let name: t => name;

/* src/Ch03/Ch03_AbstractPerson.re */
type id = int; /* (2) */
type name = string;
type t = {id, name}; /* (3) */

let id(t) = t.id;
```

```
let name(t) = t.name;
let massage(name) = String.trim(String.capitalize(name));
let make(id, name) = {id, name: massage(name)};
```

1. Now, `Ch03_AbstractPerson.t` is internally a record type just like the others, but it is exported as purely an abstract type with no implementation details *except* the operations we provide in the interface. These operations allow us to properly create `t` values and extract the person's ID and name from the `t` values.

2. We introduce two new types here: `id` and `name`, using the `type typeName = otherType;` syntax. This direct binding of a new type name to an existing type name is called a *type alias* (sometimes also called a *type abbreviation*). Type aliases don't have any influence on typechecking, but they are a useful way to document our intentions and sometimes to shorten the names of longer type names.

3. Because we aliased `id` and `name`, we can use the shortcut that Reason provides when the field and type names are the same in a record type definition, called **punning**.

Since we want to export the type aliases as well as the original types and operations, we need to repeat the same alias bindings in both the interface and the implementation. This bit of duplication allows Reason to double-check its inference against our intentions.

Zero-allocation type abstraction

Sometimes we need to enforce rules over types that already exist. For example, in `Ch03_AbstractPerson`, we have a `name` type that is just a `string`, and a `massage` function that takes a string and applies some rules to it to turn it into a "well-behaved" name. We put this type and function inside another module in a rather adhoc way, because we were focusing on the concept of "person" and its operations and not so much on "name" and its operations.

However, we don't necessarily want to make a brand-new type for names that will allocate values on top of the already-allocated name strings. We'd like to preserve our naming rules (casing and trimming) while also being cheap with memory use.

Let's extract the `name` type alias and its *smart constructor* (a `make` function that applies the rules we want to enforce when it makes values) into a dedicated module (again, note that we must define both the interface and implementation files for the module to be complete):

```
/* src/Ch03/Ch03_Person.rei */

module Name: { /* (1) */
  type t;
  let make: string => t;
  let toString: t => string;
};

type id = int; /* (2) */
type t = {id, name: Name.t}; /* (3) */

let make: (id, Name.t) => t; /* (4) */
let id: t => id;
let name: t => Name.t;

/* src/Ch03/Ch03_Person.re */
module Name = {
  type t = string; /* (5) */
  let make(string) = String.(capitalize(trim(string))); /* (6) */
  let toString(t) = t; /* (7) */
};

type id = int;
type t = {id, name: Name.t};

let make(id, name) = {id, name};
let id(t) = t.id;
let name(t) = t.name;
```

What's new here:

1. We declare a nested `Name` module with the given module type. We're telling Reason: *Ch03_Person contains a module Name that exports these items*. Note that the `Name` module's `t` type is abstract.
2. We don't make the `id` type abstract because we don't have to enforce any rules about how it should be created (we might in future though).
3. We don't need to make the `Ch03_Person.t` type abstract anymore now, because we've moved the name type and creation logic into `Name`. There's no way anyone can create the wrong `Ch03_Person.t` values because they must still go through `Name.make` to get names.

4. We make the `Ch03_Person` module functions use the `Name.t` type now.

5. The `Name.t` type is implemented as just a `string`. It will not allocate anything at runtime.

6. The `make` smart constructor will automatically enforce our rules for correct names. Also, we use the `ModuleName.(expression)` syntax here to temporarily *open* the `String` module for the scope of this one expression, bringing all its contained values into visibility. Opening modules temporarily in small scopes can be very handy to save some typing–but opening them for larger scopes can be risky because of potential name clashes.

7. Because `Name.t` is already just a `string`, *converting it back* to a `string` in `toString` entails just returning the input value.

This structuring hits a good balance:

- It exposes the `person` record-type definition so that users can examine and use their values easily
- It imposes control over a critical piece of `person` data: the name

Preventing type mix-ups

Earlier, I mentioned that we don't need to make the `id` type abstract because we don't have any rules for it right now. But there's another good reason to make a simple type abstract: preventing mix-ups between the same *physical* types (in terms of the implementation) that represent different *logical* concepts.

For example, suppose you had the following function and usage:

```
let payBill(personId, businessId) = ...;
payBill(acmeCo.id, bob.id);
```

In `Ch02_Demo` we made the ID types, for both `person` and `company`, `int`. This can backfire if we accidentally pass function arguments in the wrong order and our system tries to *pay a bill* from a company to a person.

We can prevent this kind of mix-up using a technique similar to the preceding one: make the person ID and company ID types logically distinct, while still physically representing them internally with just `int`. Here's an example:

```
/* src/Ch03/Ch03_Id.re */
module type Id = { /* (1) */
  type t;
  let make: int => t;
```

```
    let toInt: t => int;
};

module IntId = { /* (2) */
    type t = int;
    let make(int) = int;
    let toInt(t) = t;
};

module PersonId: Id = IntId; /* (3) */
module CompanyId: Id = IntId;

let bobId = PersonId.make(1); /* (4) */
let acmeCoId = CompanyId.make(1);
/*
let result = bobId == acmeCoId; /* (5) */
*/
```

In the preceding code, some very interesting things are happening:

1. We define an Id module signature, which declares an abstract t type, and a constructor and extractor function for values of t

2. We define an IntId module, with no explicit signature, which exposes a t type equal to int, and constructor and extractor functions of the same name as in the Id signature

3. We define two module aliases, PersonId and CompanyId, to IntId, and give them the explicit Id signature

4. We make PersonId.t and CompanyId.t values

5. If we tried to compare the values, we'd get a type error:

```
(Output from bsb -w)
  We've found a bug for you!
  /Users/yawar/src/learning-tydd-reason/src/Ch03/Ch03_Id.re 19:23-30
  17 | let bobId = PersonId.make(1);
  18 | let acmeCoId = CompanyId.make(1);
  19 | let result = bobId == acmeCoId;
  This has type:
    CompanyId.t
  But somewhere wanted:
    PersonId.t
```

So, Reason is able to distinguish between the two types, even though they're physically the same type, backed by the same module (Int Id), just because they were explicitly annotated with a module type (Id) that prevents Reason from "seeing" the underlying types. Because of the signature and the abstract t type, Reason can't prove that CompanyId.t and PersonId.t are the same, so trying to compare them is a type error.

Note that making these modules, even with explicit signatures, is very cheap allocation-wise:

```
// src/Ch03/Ch03_Id.bs.js
function make($$int) { return $$int; }
function toInt(t) { return t; }

var IntId = [make, toInt];
var PersonId = IntId;
var CompanyId = IntId;

var bobId = 1;
var acmeCoId = 1;
```

Reason reuses the same Int Id module and distinguishes between their types purely at compile time. We can thus elegantly separate our concerns:

- The Id signature just says that there's a t type that can be converted to and from int
- Int Id implements a module that is compatible with the Id signature but not explicitly annotated with it; thus showing that int-backed ID modules are one possible implementation of the Id signature
- The PersonId and CompanyId modules take advantage of the combination of Id and Int Id to achieve type safety by telling the compiler it can't assume that the ID types are the same (even though we know they are)

As you can see, in Reason we have a level of fine-grained power that takes advantage of the compiler to achieve very lightweight code. We will see more techniques like this in future chapters.

Summary

In this chapter, we covered how to package types and values together with modules, how to specify exactly what surface area we want to expose from our modules using signatures, and how to keep tight control over our data types using the combination of modules and signatures–even to the extent of controlling the memory allocation of data in our modules. In Reason, you'll notice this pattern a lot–you design the types to ensure that certain rules are enforced, and in a lot of situations, they will be enforced at no runtime cost.

So, stay tuned—in the next chapter, we will cover some of the most important types that we use on a daily basis in type-driven development: product types that group values together for easy access.

4
Grouping Values Together in Types

In the previous chapter, we saw a way to group types and values together so that they can be accessed under a single namespace, and we saw how these namespaces (modules) themselves have types. Modules are not, however, convenient for passing around values during runtime. We need a lightweight way to build more structured types out of simpler types, to model real-world problems.

In this chapter, we will cover these structured types, specifically:

- Record types
- Tuple types
- Object types
- JavaScript object types

Collectively, these types are referred to as **product types** because the number of possible values a product type can contain is the *product* of the number of possible values each of its component types can contain. This is an interesting result in type theory, and it gives us a hint to the fact that types obey certain algebraic laws. I will provide further reading materials on this later on in the book, after we have developed our type knowledge more.

Record types

We've used record types in several places in the book so far, mostly to build a `person` type with an ID and a name. Let's examine this simple record type a bit more closely and pick apart what exactly happens when it is created:

```
type person = {id: int, name: string};
```

As a whole, this type definition creates a new *nominal* type called `person` with two named fields: `id` and `name`, with specific `int` and `string` types. A nominal type is one that is distinguished by the typechecker from other types solely by name.

 This is as opposed to structural types, which are considered by the typechecker to be equal to their constituent types. For example, we saw in the previous chapter that modules are structurally typed. We'll see some more examples in this chapter and the next one.

At any rate, nominal types cannot be used interchangeably, even if they have the exact same definition. For example:

```
(Output from bsb -w)
  We've found a bug for you!
  /Users/yawar/src/learning-tydd-reason/src/Ch03/Ch03_Greet.re 10:20-22
   8 | type person = {id: int, name: string};
   9 | let bob = {id: 1, name: "Bob"};
  10 | let result = greet(bob);
  This has type:
    person
  But somewhere wanted:
    LearningTyddReason.Ch02_Demo.person (defined as
      LearningTyddReason.Ch02_Demo.person)
```

In the preceding error message, notice that we defined a new record type `person` in `Ch03_Greet`, created a value of this type, and tried to call the `greet` function with it. But the `greet` function only accepts `Ch02_Demo.person` values and errors on our `person` value that have the same structure but a different name (the module path is considered to be part of the name for this purpose):

Type mismatch between nominal types with the same definition

Record literals

We can create record values using the record-literal syntax:

```
/* src/Ch04/Ch04_RecordLiterals.re */
type person = {id: int, name: string};

let bob = {name: "Bob", id: 1}; /* (1) */
```

```
let jim = { /* (2) */
  let id = 2;
  let name = "Jim";
  {id, name} /* (3) */
};

let tomId = 3;
let tom = {id: tomId, name: "Tom"}; /* (4) */
```

These are the typical variations of record literals:

1. Standard record-literal syntax for a record type with the `field1` to `fieldN` fields is: `{field1: expression1, ..., fieldN: expressionN}`. Note one of the most significant things about records: *field order doesn't matter*. Here we defined a record literal with field names in the opposite order to the record-type definition.

2. We can start an enclosed scope with brackets so that the names declared inside (`id`, `name`) will not be visible from outside, and the last expression (`{id, name}`) in the enclosed scope will be the result value of the scope. Note that the scope delimiter brackets are separate from the record delimiter brackets.

3. We can use the *record field punning* syntax to write record literals when there is a name in the scope that's identical to the field name. Modern JavaScript has gained this punning feature as well.

4. We can fall back on the standard record-literal syntax with any expression if we don't have names in the scope identical to the field names.

Accessing fields and dealing with errors

Record field access syntax looks much like in other languages: `recordValue.fieldName`.

To correctly infer the types of record literals though, Reason depends on matching up the field names to record types that it knows about. A common error that you will see is when Reason can't find a suitable record type; for example, if we delete the `person` type from `Ch04_RecordLiterals`:

```
(Output from bsb -w)
  We've found a bug for you!
  /Users/yawar/src/learning-tydd-reason/src/Ch04/Ch04_RecordLiterals.re
  2:12-13
  1 | /* src/Ch04/Ch04_RecordLiterals.re */
  2 | let bob = {name: "Bob", id: 1}; /* (1) */
  3 |
  4 | let jim = { /* (2) */
  The record field name can't be found.
```

```
    If it's defined in another module or file, bring it into scope by:
    - Annotating it with said module name: let baby = {MyModule.age: 3}
    - Or specifying its type: let baby: MyModule.person = {age: 3}
```

This often happens when the record type is defined in another module. We mentioned before that Reason doesn't automatically search through other modules to find record types, because different modules could contain record types with the same field names; it would be unclear which one you meant. Instead, Reason opts to have you be explicit about the module, for example:

```
let bob = {Ch02_Demo.id: 1, name: "Bob"};
```

Now Reason can tell that:

- The id field you're referring to is in Ch02_Demo
- The record literal has only the id and name fields
- Therefore, the only type this record can possibly be is Ch02_Demo.person (it can't be Ch02_Demo.company because that record type has an employees field as well)

Changing record values

Records are by default immutable: once you create one, you can't change it. This is in addition to all Reason values being non-reassignable by default (meaning that something such as let x = 1; x = 2; is a compile error). This rigidity is for good reason: if you know that values can't change, it becomes really easy to think about each part of your program in isolation and then be confident that the parts will behave consistently when put back together. This is one of the core principles of *functional programming,* which Reason's statically typed techniques are built on.

But completely unchangeable values are not very useful. You'll usually need to change values at runtime to model the behaviors you're interested in. So Reason provides two ways to change record values: immutable updates and mutable fields.

Immutable updates

This is what we will be using most of the time. With *immutable updates,* we literally create new record values using old ones. Reason provides a special syntax for this, which comes in very handy when the record type has two or more fields. But no matter how many fields, we can always build record values by just using the normal record-literal syntax. The following are some examples:

```
/* src/Ch04/Ch04_RecordUpdates.re */
let bob = Ch04_RecordLiterals.bob;
let bobLongForm1 = {...bob, name: "Robert"}; /* (1) */
let bobLongForm2 = {Ch04_RecordLiterals.id: bob.id, name: "Robert"}; /* (2)
*/
```

Here, we update Bob's name to its long form. Note a couple of things:

1. When we use the immutable update syntax (also known in Reason as the *record spread* syntax), Reason creates a new record value that's identical to the old one (bob), except for the fields that we override. Also, even though the record type is defined in another module, we don't need to use a module prefix for any fields, because the immutable update forces Reason to look up what the fields are and thus it knows about the name field when we update it.

2. When we use the normal record-literal syntax, we need to define all the record fields. If we forget one, we'll get a rather interesting type of error:

   ```
   (Output from bsb -w)
     We've found a bug for you!
     /Users/yawar/src/learning-tydd-
   reason/src/Ch04/Ch04_RecordUpdates.re 4:20-51
     2 | let bob = Ch04_RecordLiterals.bob;
     3 | let bobLongForm1 = {...bob, name: "Robert"};
     4 | let bobLongForm2 = {Ch04_RecordLiterals.id: bob.id};
     Some record fields are undefined: name
   ```

Since Reason doesn't allow null or undefined values, it's a type error to leave out a record field:

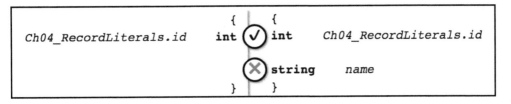

Missing record field type error

With immutable updates, we can reuse the same name and not have to worry about coming up with new names for various transformed values, thanks to shadowing:

```
let bob = Ch04_RecordLiterals.bob;
let bob = {...bob, name: "Robert"};
let bob = {...bob, id: bob.id + 1}
```

We'll often use shadowing to perform a series of updates on some value, to convey the intention that we're building or transforming the same value toward a final use.

Mutable record fields

These are used less often because they introduce an element of unsafety into a program, and force the developer to be much more defensive in their code. You have a binding of a certain value at one point, and at another point it can be a different value, and all other parts of the codebase that were behaving in a certain way based on the original value will be in for a big surprise if they happen to check again and find the new value.

Nevertheless, they can be very useful if you need some extra performance from some records, and you keep the mutations contained within the scope of a single function. Here's an example:

```
/* src/Ch04/Ch04_MutableFields.re */
type summaryStats = {
  mutable sum: float, /* (1) */
  count: int,
  mutable mean: float
};

let summarise(array) = {
  let result = {sum: 0., count: Array.length(array), mean: 0.}; /* (2) */

  for (i in 0 to result.count - 1) { /* (3) */
    result.sum = result.sum +. Array.unsafe_get(array, i); /* (4), (5) */
  };

  result.mean = result.sum /. float_of_int(result.count); /* (6), (7) */
  result
};
```

There are quite a few things going on here:

1. We make a record field mutable using the `mutable` keyword before the field name. In this case, we make only two out of the three fields mutable, because the count never needs to change for a given array.

2. We create a new record of the type with the usual literal syntax; we can use `0.` as a shorthand for `0.0` for float literals, and the `Array.length` function returns the length of a Reason array.

3. We use a `for` loop to iterate over the input array whose statistics we want. Reason fully supports imperative programming syntax, such as `for` and `while` loops; if you're looking to program in any given style, you'll likely be able to do it in Reason.

4. We sum up the array iteratively, by mutating the `sum` field. Mutating a (mutable) record field uses the simple `recordVal.field = value` syntax.

5. We get the element at the given array index using `Array.unsafe_get`, which forgoes a bounds check before getting the element. In this example, we don't need a bounds check because we've already made sure we won't go past the end of the array when we started the loop. But if we'd made a mistake, say `for (i in 0 to result.count) { ... }`, we'd get a runtime error. So it's good to be very careful with unsafe functions. There's a safe, bounds-checked syntax for array element access: `array[i]`.

6. After we finish iterating through the entire array, we mutate the `mean` field to the final mean value.

7. We can't divide the float `sum` by the int `count`, so we need to convert the int `count` to a float. Note that we don't go the other way round, that is, convert the float `sum` to an int, because that would be a lossy conversion!

Note how overall we are keeping the mutation inside the bounds of a single function. Although, this mutation safety is somewhat undermined by just returning the `summaryStats` value with two mutable fields to the caller. In future mutation examples, we'll show safer usage patterns.

 We're using slightly different operators for float arithmetic: in Reason, integer and float arithmetic are completely separate and they don't mix. The float arithmetic operators are the same as the integer arithmetic ones, except with a "." appended to them. The Reason philosophy is very much one of *explicit is better than implicit*.

To reiterate, for most purposes, immutable records work very well indeed. Mutable record fields come in handy in a limited set of situations, and when we do use them, we need to take extra precautions against accidental mutations.

Record patterns

In Chapter 2, *Program with Types and Values*, we saw that the general syntax for value bindings is:

```
let PATTERN = VALUE;
```

This syntax applies to records too, because record literals also act as patterns. In the case of record patterns, we call it *destructuring pattern matching*, because we bind names by matching against the structure of the record value and pulling out its fields. Here are some examples:

```
/* src/Ch04/Ch04_RecordPatterns.re */
open Ch04_RecordLiterals; /* (1) */

let {id: bobId, name: bobName} = bob; /* (2) */
let {id, name: jimName} = jim; /* (3) */
let {id: tomId, name: _} = tom; /* (4) */
let {name, _} = tom; /* (5) */
let {name: tomName} = tom; /* (6) */
```

These are the possible variations of record patterns:

1. We globally open the record literals module, to get convenient access to the types and values defined there, without having to qualify every time. I didn't show this in the previous chapter because I deliberately wanted to de-emphasize global openings since they are usually more risky. In controlled cases such as this one though, they are OK.
2. Record patterns look just like record literals, except what would be the field values are also names (bobId, bobName) and these names get bound to the actual values in the record.
3. We can use a shortcut if we want to bind a name that's the same as the field name: just omit the colon and field value on the right. We can even mix the two styles.

4. We can bind only some fields of a record to values, and explicitly not bind the other fields by binding them to the underscore symbol, which means ignore.

5. We can bind some fields to names and unreservedly ignore the rest using the underscore symbol.

6. We can bind some fields and ignore the rest by completely omitting them. Reason will infer the type of the pattern using the field names it sees but may get confused if there are multiple record types defined with the same fields.

As you can see, the record-pattern syntax is very sophisticated and detailed, built up over time as Reason's base language, OCaml, has been in active industrial use. It will take a little time to get used to all the patterns; start simple and use the more succinct ones as needed.

One last thing to mention about record patterns: they are also irrefutable patterns, just like simple value bindings, such as `let x = 1;`. Irrefutability simply means that once a pattern is compiled, there is no way it can fail to match against the value on the right-hand side at runtime. By this metric, record patterns pass because binding them is just a matter of binding their fields to names, and simple name bindings are also irrefutable. But we will see examples of refutable patterns in the next chapter, so keep an eye out for them.

Tuple types

Tuples are lightweight, structural types. To be precise, they are types made up of other types, joined together within parentheses in a particular order, separated by commas, and without field names. The tuple value syntax is very simple–open parenthesis, comma-separated list of values, close parenthesis. In fact, the value syntax closely mimics the type of the tuples themselves.

 Tuple pronunciation varies depending on who you ask, but I usually pronounce it to rhyme with *couple*.

Why would we use tuples when we have record types with field names? Sometimes, we don't want to spin up a new type, with a definition, just to hold some values together. Tuples are a low-ceremony way to do that. But the danger of using them over larger portions of a codebase is that they're not self-describing like record types are. Here's an example:

```
/* src/Ch04/Ch04_Tuples.re */

/* ID, name */
let bob = (1, "Bob");

/* Name, ID */
let jim = ("Jim", 2);

/*let bobEqualsJim = bob == jim; */
```

 I used just two values to make up the tuples here, but Reason supports tuples of any size.

Notice the last line, which is commented out. If we uncomment that line, we'll get the following error:

```
(Output from bsb -w)
  We've found a bug for you!
  /Users/yawar/src/learning-tydd-reason/src/Ch04/Ch04_Tuples.re 4:27-29
  2 | let bob = (1, "Bob");
  3 | let jim = ("Jim", 2);
  4 | let bobEqualsJim = bob == jim;
  This has type:
    (string, int)
  But somewhere wanted:
    (int, string)
  The incompatible parts:
    string
    vs
    int
```

 I removed the descriptive comments to fit all the code in the error message.

The type error tells us the types of the two tuples, and we see that they differ purely by the ordering of their component types:

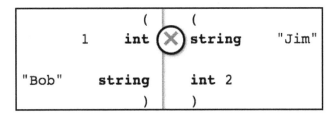

Tuple type mismatch error

In the preceding error, we also see that Reason doesn't bother to check the entire type once it finds even one error in the structure of the tuple types. Nine times out of ten, as soon as we investigate this error message, we'll immediately see the problem–the values are swapped and so are the types–and fix it in one go. The other time, we'll hit another type error after we fix the first one, and fix that. I like to think of type-driven development as really *type-error-driven development* because hitting type errors is a really good scenario as it means one more potential bug that the production code will never see.

Accessing tuple values

We can access values inside tuples in two main ways: destructuring pattern matching and accessor functions.

Destructuring pattern matching

We can bind names to values in tuples using destructuring, similar to records:

```
let (bobId, bobName) = bob;
let (jimName, _) = jim;
```

The general pattern is (field1, field2, ..., fieldN) for *N*-tuples. As always, the special _ pattern allows us to disregard fields we don't care about. Unlike with records, though, we can't omit them altogether–we must list out all the fields separated by commas. Because tuples are typed according to their structure, omitting a tuple field changes the type we'd be matching against and would be a type error:

```
(Output from bsb -w)
  We've found a bug for you!
  /Users/yawar/src/learning-tydd-reason/src/Ch04/Ch04_Tuples.re 12:18-20
  10 |
  11 | let tom = (3, "Tom", 45); /* ID, name, age */
  12 | let (tomId, _) = tom;
  This has type:
    (int, string, int)
  But somewhere wanted:
    ('a, 'b)
```

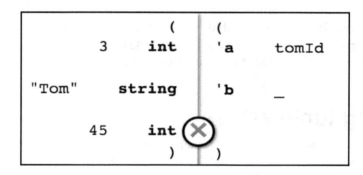

Tuple destructure type error

We're seeing two interesting types here: 'a and 'b (usually pronounced *alpha* and *beta*). We'll delve into what they mean in a future chapter, but right now we can think of them as Reason's way of saying *I haven't figured out these types yet*. In any case, notice that they don't trigger the actual type error–since Reason doesn't know what they are, it can't assume that they're type mismatches. What really causes the error is the missing third element of the tuple. Effectively, we're trying to match a 3-tuple against a 2-tuple, and this triggers the type error.

Accessor functions

Reason provides two convenience functions, `fst` and `snd`, to get the first and second positional values from tuples. Here's an example:

```
let bobId = fst(bob);
let jimId = snd(jim);
```

These functions often come in handy when we're trying to manage lots of tuples and need to tell other functions how to manipulate them. We'll see an example of this kind of controlled behavior in the upcoming chapter on functions.

Object types

Objects are part of OCaml's full-fledged support for **object-oriented programming** (**OOP**). They combine some of the best properties of records and tuples: they are structural so we can create them in an adhoc way (without having to define their types), and we can provide field names (in OOP terminology, methods) that act as descriptive names. Here's an example:

```
/* src/Ch04/Ch04_Objects.re */
let bob = {as _; pub id = 1; pub name = "Bob"}; /* (1), (2) */

let greet(person) =
  "Hello, " ++
  person#name ++
  " with ID " ++
  string_of_int(person#id); /* (3) */

let jim = {
  pub id = 2;
  pub name = "Jim";
  pub sayHi = "Hi, my name is " ++ this#name /* (4) */
};

Js.log(greet(jim)); /* (5) */
/*Js.log(greet({as _; pub name = "Tom"}));*/
```

These show some basic usage of Reason objects:

1. Objects are delimited by brackets and can refer to themselves within the brackets using the `this` keyword. However, if we don't use `this`, Reason will warn us about an unused value. So we can optionally ignore it using `as _` at the start of the object to suppress this warning.
2. We can create objects in an adhoc way by specifying their public methods (that is, fields) using the `pub` keyword. Reason will infer the type of the object from its public methods.
3. We can access object fields (that is, call their public methods) using the `#` notation. Also, in this case, we need to convert the int ID to a string to concatenate it to other strings.
4. We can call methods on the current object by using `this`.
5. If we load the output JavaScript module, `src/Ch04/Ch04_Objects.bs.js`, in NodeJS, Jim's greeting will be printed.

If you look at the JavaScript output, you'll see that it's fairly complex. Reason objects are indeed fairly heavyweight values because they can contain a lot of functionality wrapped up inside them. Often, we don't need this level of power because we have other ways of modeling data and behavior. We'll cover more abstraction techniques in further chapters that lessen the need for Reason objects.

Inheritance and subtyping

You may be wondering whether Reason objects support inheritance. In fact, they do fully support inheritance with runtime dispatch. We won't delve into inheritance because OOP style is not the focus of this book; you can find ample resources for OOP in the Reason and OCaml documentation (they have equivalent functionality, just with different syntax).

The one thing we need to emphasize is that Reason objects are *extensible* in a specific way, using a typing technique called **row polymorphism**. This is an advanced topic, and we'll cover different kinds of *polymorphism* (giving different types of common behaviors) in a future chapter. However, the basic idea is that a u object that supports a *superset* of all the methods of a t object is considered to have a U type that is a *subtype* of the T type of the t object. So, the u object can be safely **upcast** to the T type (that is, we can safely say that u has the T type) because that would not be a lossy conversion. In other words, objects support *inheritance* simply in terms of their method implementations.

Let's look at a concrete example: the `greet` function in the preceding example code. We call it with the `jim` object. The function calls two methods on its input object: `id` and `name`. Reason actually infers the input object type as `{.. id: int, name: string}`. We call this an open object type. The *openness* is marked by the two dots right after the opening bracket. It means we can call `greet` with subtypes of this type.

In fact, we do just that, on the line marked `(5)`: we call `greet` with `jim`, which is an object with the `id`, `name`, and `sayHi` methods. In other words, it's a subtype of the type that `greet` is expecting, and `greet` accepts it because its input parameter type allows subtypes. If you change the call to use `bob`, it will succeed as well because `bob` also conforms to the type that has `id` and `name` methods of the expected types.

However, if you uncomment the last line, you'll get the following type error:

```
(Output from bsb -w)
  We've found a bug for you!
  /Users/yawar/src/learning-tydd-reason/src/Ch04/Ch04_Objects.re 17:14-37
  15 |
  16 |   Js.log(greet(jim)); /* (5) */
  17 |   Js.log(greet({as _; pub name = "Tom"}));
  This has type:
    {. name : string }
  But somewhere wanted:
    {.. id : int, name : string }
  The first object type has no method id
```

This error indicates that we're passing in an input that doesn't meet the minimum requirements for the `greet` function. Indeed, intuitively we can see that the input only has a `name` method, whereas the `greet` function requires both the `id` and `name` methods.

If you think about it, Reason objects behave very much like JavaScript, Python, or Ruby objects, in the sense that we can treat them as bags of values and methods. The only difference is Reason checks the methods for us at compile time instead of runtime!

JavaScript object types

The first thing to explain about JavaScript objects in Reason is that they're not actually JavaScript objects, they are Reason syntactic constructs that will compile down to JavaScript objects. We use the latter term as a shortcut to refer to the former.

With the realization that Reason objects behave a lot like JavaScript objects, we can understand how Reason's support for JavaScript objects works. This support is baked in, but only if we're targeting JavaScript using BuckleScript. In this project, we are, so here's an example:

```
/* src/Ch04/Ch04_JsObjects.re */
let bob = {"id": 1, "name": "Bob"}; /* (1) */

let greet (person) =
  "Hello, " ++
  person##name ++
  " with ID " ++
  string_of_int (person##id); /* (2) */

let jim = {"id": 2, "name": "Jim", "age": 29}; /* (3) */

Js.log (greet (jim));
```

This example shows some typical JavaScript object usage:

1. Notice how similar the JavaScript object literal is to actual JavaScript. It's explicitly designed this way–enclosed in brackets, field names in double-quotes, values following the colon.
2. The JavaScript object field access looks almost exactly like the Reason object method calls, only substituting # with ##.
3. It's possible to give JavaScript objects actual methods that refer to the this JavaScript value, but it's a very advanced topic, so we're using an age field here instead.

Notice at the end that, just like with the Reason objects example, we're passing in an object (jim) that exposes a superset of the fields required by the greet function. This is why we use this special syntax in Reason to model JavaScript objects: they act like Reason objects in the sense of supporting subtyping with row polymorphism. With this subtyping, we can model many JavaScript idioms with an ease that we just couldn't do with the simpler record types. The preceding use of the greet function is just one example of that, and, indeed in the JavaScript world, it's common to see objects passed around between functions that use only some subset of their properties.

If you look at the JavaScript output, notice that it is comparatively very simple–it really is just simple JavaScript object manipulation. Thanks to BuckleScript's ability to model JavaScript objects using basic OCaml objects, and Reason's nice object syntax, we get the best of both worlds.

We won't, as a rule, focus on JavaScript object types in this book, but in real-world Reason usage it's very good to understand how they work.

Summary

In this chapter, we thoroughly explored some of the most important types Reason has to offer: product types, such as records, tuples, objects, and JavaScript objects. By understanding what they are and how and when to use them, we can now model a large portion of our data-processing needs.

In the next chapter, we'll cover sum types, which are the flip side of the coin from product types, allowing us to model alternatives directly in our data.

5
Putting Alternative Values in Types

In the previous chapter, we saw how to build values that capture multiple types of values together, and the different ways that we can build those types. This lets us say that we have a value of the composite (product) type only if we have *all* of the values of their composed types. Sometimes though, we need values that must be *only one* type out of several types.

In this chapter, we will cover these *only one* types, namely:

- Variant types
- Polymorphic variant types
- Generalized algebraic data types

Collectively, these types are known as *sum types* because the number of possible values that a sum type can contain is the *sum* of the number of possible values of each of its component types. We'll see how this is true in this chapter!

Variant types

Variant types are Reason's simple, idiomatic sum types. You can think of them as similar to enums (a limited set of values that are declared to form a type) from other languages, only more powerful because each *variant case* (possible alternative value) can optionally carry a payload inside it. Here's an example:

```
/* src/Ch05/Ch05_Variants.re */
type education = School | College | Postgrad | Other; /* (1) */

type poNumber = string;
type paymentMethod = Cash | PurchaseOrder(poNumber); /* (2) */

let bobEducation = College; /* (3) */
```

```
let bobPaymentMethod = Cash;
let jimEducation = Other;
let jimPaymentMethod = PurchaseOrder("PO-1234"); /* (4) */
```

This module defines some types for storing someone's education level and a payment method of either cash or purchase order:

1. Variant type definitions start with `type typeName =` just like any other type of definition, and have one or more *variant constructors* (also known as *data constructors*) on the right-hand side of the equals sign. These constructors all have the exact same type and can be used as literal values.

2. Variant constructors must start with an uppercase letter and can each carry any number of payloads, as defined within parentheses. This can be a comma-separated list of types that will make up the payload. Here we defined the `poNumber` type instead of just using `string` directly, to make the code more self-documenting.

3. We can use variant cases directly as literal values. Now, `bobEducation` has the type `education`.

4. For variant constructors that carry payloads, we can pass them in as a comma-separated list between parentheses, a syntax that mirrors their definition.

The first variant type, `education`, is a simple one that we can find in a lot of languages. It just defines an allowed set of values for a person's education. Of course, this may not be realistic in all scenarios, but sometimes we just need types to be realistic enough to model our problem.

The next variant type, `paymentMethod`, is the really interesting one. It's saying that valid payment methods are cash or a purchase order with a PO number. Note that for cash we don't need any extra info, but for a purchase order we require its number; it's impossible to describe a PO with a corresponding number.

Let's think about this for a second. To represent a payment method in other languages, you might do something like the following:

```
// JavaScript
const bobPaymentMethod = {type: 'PaymentMethod.Cash'};
const jimPaymentMethod =
{
  type: 'PaymentMethod.PurchaseOrder',
  poNumber: 'PO-1234'
};
```

Notice the problem? Nothing's stopping us from creating objects with `type`: `'PaymentMethod.Cash'` and a `poNumber` property, or even worse, `type`: `'PaymentMethod.PurchaseOrder'` and no `poNumber` property. We'd have no static guarantees that purchase orders would always have an associated ID. Variant types give us this static guarantee.

Pattern matching

We can construct variant values easily enough—just type in the variant constructors and give them any data they need. But variants really shine when we work with their values.

For example, suppose you want to write a function that returns a thank you message for any given payment. Part of the message will hinge on the payment method:

```
/* src/Ch05/Ch05_PatternMatching.re */
type paymentMethod = Ch05_Variants.paymentMethod = /* (1) */
| Cash
| PurchaseOrder(Ch05_Variants.poNumber);

let paymentMethodThanks(paymentMethod) = switch (paymentMethod) { /* (2) */
| Cash => "Thank you for your cash payment"
| PurchaseOrder(poNumber) =>
  "Thank you for your purchase order # " ++ poNumber
};
```

We will introduce some new syntax here:

1. We use a **type equation** to tell the compiler that this variant type defined in this module is the same as the other variant type defined in `Ch05_Variants`, and crucially that its constructors are also exactly the same.
2. We **pattern match** on the given payment method using Reason's `switch` expression, which can **destructure** data that can match against patterns.

We could have simply redefined the variant type in both modules; but variant types in Reason are nominal (that is, even the same variant type definition is considered a distinct type if it's in a different module) unless we use a type equation. In this simple example it's not critical that the compiler equates the two types, but sometimes in a Reason codebase, you'll want to *bring in* the variant constructors from another module for ease of access. Otherwise, you'll need to either open the other module (risky) or prefix the constructors with the modules (verbose), for example, `Ch05_Variants.Cash`.

The power of switch

In the previous section, we saw how to use the `switch` expression. But that barely scratched the surface of what `switch` can do. Switch expressions match against arbitrary patterns and evaluate the branch that corresponds to the *first* matching pattern.

Here's a slightly more formal syntax for a switch expression:

```
switch (expr) {
| pat1 => res1
| pat2 => res2
...
| patN => resN
}
```

This entire syntactic form evaluates to a single value. Each subsection of the expression that starts with a bar character (`|`) is called a **branch**.

The steps for evaluating the expression are as follows:

1. Evaluate `expr`.
2. Match the value of `expr` against `pat1`; if it matches, evaluate the entire expression to `res1` and ignore all the other branches.
3. Otherwise, continue matching the value against each pattern in turn, and evaluate to the first result that corresponds to the matching pattern.
4. If none of the patterns match, throw a runtime error (called an exception), `Match_failure`.

Each branch of the expression must have the same return type for it to compile. Note that the order of the branches may or may not be important, depending on what kind of patterns we're matching. If we're matching against a variant type's exact cases, order is not important because variant cases naturally don't have any concept of *ordering*. That is, even if we defined `Cash` before `PurchaseOrder` in the `paymentMethod` type definition, that doesn't mean that `Cash` is intrinsically *less* than `PurchaseOrder`. There is no precedence.

However, patterns don't have to be variant cases. They can be any valid combination of names and literal values. In this context, a name is anything that is a valid Reason identifier, such as `age` or `_123`. Literal values include variant cases, but also values of basic types such as `char`, `string`, `int`, `float`, and so on; and also tuples and record values. If a pattern matches against the input expression, any names it contains get *bound* to the relevant parts of the expression and are made available in the scope of the result expression on the right-hand side of the `=>`.

With name binding, literal values, and ordering, patterns can get quite sophisticated; let's see a few examples:

```
/* src/Ch05/Ch05_PatternMatchOrder.re */
type person = Ch04_RecordLiterals.person = {id: int, name: string};

let classifyId(id) = switch (id) {
| 1 | 2 | 3 | 4 | 5 => "Low" /* (1) */
| 6 | 7 | 8 | 9 | 10 => "Medium"
| _ => "High"
};

let greet1(person) = switch (person.id, person.name) { /* (2) */
| (_, "Dave") => "I'm sorry, Dave, I can't let you do that."
| (1, _) => "Hello, boss."
| (id, name) => "Hi, " ++ name ++ " with ID " ++ string_of_int(id) ++ "!"
};

let greet2(person) = switch (person) {
| {name: "Dave"} => "I'm sorry, Dave, I can't let you do that." /* (3) */
| {id: 1} => "Hello, boss."
| {id, name} => "Hi, " ++ name ++ " with ID " ++ string_of_int(id) ++ "!"
};
```

There are a few interesting things here:

1. We're switching on an `int` ID, listing multiple alternative patterns on a single line, separated by bars. Patterns are in fact recursively defined; this means that patterns can contain more patterns! In other words, we can combine several individual patterns, such as 1, 2, and so on, with the vertical bar to indicate that any of these should match. This is called an **or pattern**. Note that the ordering of the patterns means that at runtime, the input ID will first be checked against the numbers 1 to 5, and only then with the other patterns. In this pattern match, the underscore symbol (_) means *anything, I don't care and don't bind the value*.

2. Given a `person` value, we switch on its name and ID. We're actually switching on a single expression; the expression `(person.id, person.name)` is a tuple that we create on the spot and match against immediately. The really interesting thing here is the ordering of the patterns. We're expressing the logic that we always show a special message for Dave, and if it's not Dave and if it's someone with ID 1, we greet them as the boss, and only if it's not Dave or the boss, we greet the person by name and ID.

3. In `greet2`, we switch on the `person` directly using record literal patterns and express the same ordered logic as before, only this time we don't need to construct a temporary tuple since we know we can pattern match directly against records. There's not necessarily a performance benefit to this, but you may find the code slightly neater–it's subjective.

Pattern matching can handle quite sophisticated data structures, because of the special property of patterns that they are *composable*. However, with this great power come two warnings: first, we need to understand the order in which we list the branches of our switch expressions so that we don't get unexpected results; second, we need to avoid potential runtime errors arising from the use of refutable patterns.

Refutable patterns

It's important to understand that the `switch` expression is one form of pattern matching in Reason, out of three:

- Switch expression
- Let binding (see `Chapter 2`, *Program with Types and Values*)
- Function arguments (we'll cover functions in a future chapter)

With all three forms of pattern matching, we run the risk of runtime errors if we use refutable patterns incorrectly. *Refutable patterns* are patterns that type-check, but could *potentially* fail at runtime. Here are a couple of simple examples:

```
let 3 = 3;
let getPoNumber(paymentMethod) =
{
   let PurchaseOrder(poNumber) = paymentMethod;
   poNumber
};
```

Surprised by `let 3 = 3`? Remember that the left-hand side of the equals sign can be any pattern–even a single literal value! Also, let `PurchaseOrder(poNumber) = ...` is a destructuring of a variant case, not a function definition. The difference is the case of the first letter, `P`. Remember that Reason modules and data constructors start with an uppercase letter, while types and values start with a lowercase letter.

If you try the first binding, you'll see the following warning:

```
(Output from bsb -w)
  Warning number 8
  /Users/yawar/src/learning-tydd-reason/src/Ch05/Ch05_PatternMatchOrder.re
22:5
  20 | };
  21 |
  22 | let 3 = 3;
  You forgot to handle a possible value here, for example:
0
```

It's not really obvious what the problem is: the value being bound is literally 3, it could never be 0, so how could we forget to handle it? The thing to realize is that the compiler looks only at the types–it sees that we used a refutable pattern of type int, and warns us about the simplest int that it knows we didn't handle: 0.

If you try the second:

```
(Output from bsb -w)
  Warning number 8
  /Users/yawar/src/learning-tydd-
reason/src/Ch05/Ch05_VariantPatternMatching.re 13:7-29
  11 |
  12 | let getPoNumber(paymentMethod) = {
  13 |   let PurchaseOrder(poNumber) = paymentMethod;
  14 |   poNumber
  15 | };
  You forgot to handle a possible value here, for example:
Cash
```

This time, it's quite obvious: at runtime, the getPoNumber function could get called with the Cash value (because that type-checks!) but it doesn't know how to handle it. There's nothing it can do but throw a runtime error. The compiler figures this out in the same way as before, by looking at the paymentMethod type and looking for values of the type that it knows weren't handled.

This feature that checks if we handled all possible patterns of any given type is called **exhaustivity checking** and is one of the most powerful and useful features of Reason's type system. It's also present in a few languages that are either derived from the same ML (Meta Language) heritage as Reason or took inspiration from it. No matter what language, if you have exhaustivity checking at your disposal, try to use it as much as possible because it's a great safety net.

The when clause and general branching

Not only do switch expressions pattern match on their inputs, but they can also add a general test condition called a when **clause** to the end of each pattern. This lets you check completely general conditions in each branch to match against that branch. Note that using a when clause does give up exhaustivity checking, though, so before reaching for it, think about if you can do without. Sometimes, you just can't. For example:

```
/* src/Ch05/Ch05_Branching.re */
type education = Ch05_Variants.education = /* (1) */
| School
| College
| Postgrad
| Other;

type paymentMethod = Ch05_Variants.paymentMethod =
| Cash
| PurchaseOrder(Ch05_Variants.poNumber);

/** Returns purchase order IDs that start with 'ACME', otherwise
    nothing. */
let getAcmeOrder(paymentMethod) = switch (paymentMethod) {
| PurchaseOrder(poNumber)
  /* (2),                                    (3) */
  when String.sub(poNumber, 0, 4) == "ACME" => Some(poNumber)
| _ => None /* (4) */
};

let decidePaymentMethod(orderTotal, orderId) =
 if (orderTotal <= 50.0) Cash /* (5) */
 else PurchaseOrder("PO-" ++ orderId);
```

This code sample shows a scenario for using a when clause:

1. We redefine the types we need and equate them for interoperability. Strictly speaking, in this case, we didn't need to do that. But in most real-world code, you would.
2. We add a when clause to the PurchaseOrder(poNumber) base pattern to check that the PO number starts with the word ACME. This is something we can't do with pattern matching because we can't match against parts of strings.
3. We also evaluate the branch to a Some(poNumber). Some is a built-in data constructor that expresses the idea that *there is a value here (as opposed to no value).* It actually accepts *any* type, not just a string, and we'll see how that works in the next chapter.

4. The case where the PO number doesn't start with the word ACME evaluates to None, which is the same type as Some (whatever), but it expresses the idea that *there's no value here*. The type of Some (whatever) and None is a variant type option (whateverType), and it's very useful for safely passing around values that might not logically exist. In this case, it's useful for our function getAcmeOrder because, given any payment method at runtime, it might not actually contain an ACME purchase order, so we need a way to say *it's not an ACME PO*, and None gives us that.

5. Reason also has a traditional if-else syntax, which is also an expression and evaluates to a value. Both the if and else branches must evaluate to values of the same type; if we leave out the else branch, it's assumed to evaluate to () of type unit. In Reason, ()—pronounced *unit*—roughly means the same thing that void means in C, C++, and so on, except that it's an actual assignable value and it can come in handy sometimes. In the case of if expressions, concretely this means that we should either include an else clause or ensure that the if clause evaluates to type unit. Typically, this happens with functions that carry out an action and don't evaluate to a useful value, for example, Js.log("Hello").

 So far in this book, we've seen a couple of types that look like typeName(typeParam), but we haven't delved into what they are or how they work. In the next chapter, we'll learn about parameterized types and how they can help write safe, reusable code.

Stricter safety checks

It's worth digressing a bit to the compiler's exhaustivity check warning. As you'll recall, it looks as follows:

```
(Output from bsb -w)
Warning number 8
/Users/yawar/src/learning-tydd-reason/src/Ch05/Ch05_Branching.re 25:5
23 |    else PurchaseOrder("PO-" ++ orderId);
24 |
25 | let 3 = 3;
You forgot to handle a possible value here, for example:
0
```

The problem with a compile warning is that it doesn't fail the compile. We can end up with code running in production that type-checked, but is not actually type-safe, because it forgot to handle some corner case. It would really be ideal if we could tell the compiler to fail the compile if it finds any non-exhaustive patterns, so we can rule out shipping them to production.

Fortunately, we can tell the compiler to *promote* a warning to an error. In our case, since we're using a BuckleScript project, we can edit the `bsconfig.json` file slightly:

```json
// bsconfig.json
{
  // ... rest of the file ...
  "warnings":
  {
    "error": "+8"
  }
}
```

After editing the file, we can restart `bsb -w` to have the new setting take effect. The `"warnings"` property contains an object with potentially a couple of properties, one of which is an `"error"` property that has a corresponding string value listing the warning numbers that we want to promote into errors with the `"+NUM"` syntax. We can get the exact number from the compiler warning message (see preceding snippet).

Now, this same warning will fail the compile:

```
(Output from bsb -w)
  Warning number 8
  /Users/yawar/src/learning-tydd-reason/src/Ch05/Ch05_Branching.re 25:5
  23 |    else PurchaseOrder("PO-" ++ orderId);
  24 |
  25 | let 3 = 3;
  You forgot to handle a possible value here, for example:
0

  We've found a bug for you!
  /Users/yawar/src/learning-tydd-reason/src/Ch05/Ch05_Branching.re
  Some fatal warnings were triggered (1 occurrences)
```

Now the compiler will stop the compiling when it encounters a *fatal warning* and we can enjoy safer pattern matching.

Polymorphic variant types

While Reason's variant types are conceptually simple, much of their power comes from the ability to use them with pattern matching and exhaustivity checking. Reason also provides a more powerful, but also more complex sum type, called **polymorphic variants**. As the name suggests, these variants are more flexible than regular variants. Here are a few things that we can do with polymorphic variants, but not with regular variants:

- Create values without defining the types beforehand, letting the compiler infer the type
- Compose multiple sets of variant cases together
- Define functions that handle *at least* a set of variant cases as input
- Define functions that output *at most* a set of variant cases as output

In a sense, we can think of polymorphic variants as being related to regular variants in the same way that objects are related to records. They are, in fact, structural types in the same way that objects and modules are because the compiler infers the types of values by inspecting their structures.

Creating and typing values

Let's see a few examples to get a feel for how polymorphic variants work:

```
/* src/Ch05/Ch05_PolymorphicVariantBasics.re */
let colour = `Red; /* (1) */
let angle = `degrees(45.0); /* (2) */

type event = [ /* (3) */
| `clickTap(int, int) /* x, y */
| `keypress(char)
| `pointerMove(int, int, int, int) /* x1, y1, x2, y2 */
];

type mobileEvent = [
| event /* (4) */
| `deviceShake(int) /* how many times */
| `accel(float) /* m/s^2 */
];

let pressA: mobileEvent = `keypress('a'); /* (5) */
/* let shakeThrice: event = `deviceShake(3); /* (6) */ */
```

There's a lot of new syntaxes here, but hopefully it should look somewhat similar to regular variant syntax:

1. We can define an adhoc polymorphic variant value and let the compiler figure out its type. In this case, the editor support should show us a type [> `Red]. This means a polymorphic variant type that has at least the `Red data constructor that I've seen, and possibly more. The brackets ([...]) around the type syntactically distinguish it from regular variants and also suggest that we should think of it as like a bounded set.

2. Polymorphic variant constructors can contain payloads just like regular variant constructors. Also, unlike regular constructors, polymorphic constructors can start with a lowercase letter. This is still unambiguous though because polymorphic variant constructors must always be prefixed with a back-tick character.

3. We can explicitly define polymorphic variant types using the syntax shown. Note that the compiler doesn't automatically infer any later values that use the defined constructors as being of the defined type. I'll explain this a bit more in the *fifth* point.

4. Polymorphic variant types can compose other polymorphic variant types and become an expanded set of cases. This lets us model cases that can be considered part of the set (type), but can also be considered separately, for example, device input events.

5. We must explicitly annotate a value with a polymorphic variant type to tell the compiler that it must be *exactly* this type. Without this annotation, within the module the compiler will infer the type from the structure of the data constructor, that is, in this case [> `keypress(char)]. Note that declaring the exact types of the polymorphic variant values in module signatures will work, but only from the point of view of other modules, not internally within the module. Usually, that's good enough!

6. We can't declare that a polymorphic variant constructor has some type if that type doesn't actually declare the constructor first. Here's what the error would look like:

```
(Output from bsb -w)
  We've found a bug for you!
  /Users/yawar/src/learning-tydd-
reason/src/Ch05/Ch05_PolymorphicVariantBasics.re 18:26-40
  16 |
  17 | let pressA: mobileEvent = `keypress('a'); /* (5) */
  18 | let shakeThrice: event = `deviceShake(3); /* (6) */
  This has type:
    [> `deviceShake(int) ]
```

```
But somewhere wanted:
    event
The second variant type does not allow tag(s) `deviceShake
```

We can visualize the error as follows:

```
        [>         [
`deviceShake(int) (X)
                   | `clickTap(int, int)
                   | `keypress(char)
                   | `pointerMove(int, int, int, int)
        ]          ]
```

Polymorphic variant type mismatch

Inputting values into functions

Now that we can create polymorphic variant values, let's do something useful with them.
How can we handle a value that we get at runtime? It turns out, the same way we'd handle
a normal variant: pattern matching:

```
/* src/Ch05/Ch05_PolymorphicVariantInputs.re */
let eventToString(event) = switch (event) {
| `clickTap(x, y) => {j|`clickTap($x, $y)|j} /* (1), (2) */
| `keypress(char) => {j|`keypress($char)|j}
| `pointerMove(x1, y1, x2, y2) => {j|`pointerMove($x1, $y1, $x2, $y2)|j}
| `deviceShake(times) => {j|`deviceShake($times)|j}
| `accel(mssq) => {j|`accel($mssq)|j}
};

/* (3) */
let pressAString = eventToString(Ch05_PolymorphicVariantBasics.pressA);

/* (4) */
let `degrees(angleVal) = Ch05_PolymorphicVariantBasics.angle;
```

1. We can pattern match on an input polymorphic variant data constructor the
   same way we'd match against a regular constructor: by writing out the
   constructor as a pattern and binding any of its contained data that we want to
   use.

2. We use a BuckleScript-specific string interpolation syntax for convenience here: {j| ... $name ... |j}. The name must be in scope, and it must be only a name, not an arbitrary expression such as 1 + 2. The {j| and |j} act as string delimiters and can be used for multiline and Unicode string literals as well.

3. We can call the function with any value that conforms to its inferred input type, which pressA does because we made sure both its type and our new function have the same polymorphic variant cases.

4. We can as usual pattern match directly with a let-binding, but notice that there's no exhaustivity warning here. The compiler now doesn't know what other cases there might be, so it doesn't warn us. For this reason, it's best to avoid let-binding pattern matching of polymorphic variant values.

Understanding polymorphic variant inference

If you have type hinting enabled in your editor, it should tell you that the type of eventToString is as follows:

```
[<
| `accel('a)
| `clickTap('b, 'c)
| `deviceShake('d)
| `keypress('e)
| `pointerMove('f, 'g, 'h, 'i)
] =>
string
```

The compiler alphabetizes the variant cases when printing them out, but just like with regular variants, the cases don't have any intrinsic ordering.

This function type is divided into two main parts: the input on the left of the arrow, and the output on the right. The input is a polymorphic variant type that can contain any of the listed cases or less, and these cases can have payloads in the given positions. Notice that the payloads all have types that look like 'x, that is, starting with an apostrophe character. As we mentioned before, this character means that this type will be filled in later. Specifically, it's known as a type parameter.

The most important thing to understand about this inferred function type is that the input polymorphic variant is given an upper bound (<), meaning this function can handle a polymorphic variant type that has these cases, and also polymorphic variant types that have a *subset* of these cases, but it certainly can't handle any *more* cases.

Now, let's tackle the reason why all the payload types are going to be filled in later. We already know that they're just ints and floats. Why couldn't the compiler figure that out?

It turns out that when we used the payloads in BuckleScript's special string interpolation syntax sugar, the compiler was never told what their exact types were. String interpolation just lets us stuff anything in a JavaScript string, without having to be specific to the compiler as we usually would, for example, with a string concatenation such as `"Hello"` `++ " world"`. This is very convenient for producing output, but can lead to pitfalls where the compiler can't infer a type; so it's good to be aware of this.

Overall, notice the important safety property we achieve that's very similar to the type safety of objects: we can (to a certain extent) use adhoc variant constructors safely with the compiler's help.

Outputting values from functions

What if we want to go in the opposite direction? That is, output polymorphic variant values from functions:

```
/* src/Ch05/Ch05_PolymorphicVariantOutputs.re */
let stringToColour(string) = switch (string) {
| "red" => `red
| "green" => `green
| "blue" => `blue
| _ => `unknown /* we need to handle the edge case */
};
```

This time, two interesting things happen:

- The compiler does exhaustivity checking on the input, which is a string, so we need to handle *all* possible string inputs (the last one is the catch-all)
- The compiler swaps the polymorphic variant type's bound, making the type (of the function):

```
string => [> `blue | `green | `red | `unknown]
```

This time, the compiler infers a *lower bound* for the polymorphic variant return type, because it seems that the function returns those cases and it may potentially return more, but it will certainly never return *fewer* cases.

Polymorphic variant types are a deep and powerful part of Reason, and we'll explore them a bit more in the coming chapters.

Generalized algebraic data types

Generalized algebraic data types (**GADTs**) are another deep and powerful area of the language. As with polymorphic variant types, much of their true power is exposed when they're used with type parameters. But we can understand their surface syntax and how they relate to regular variant types, for now.

GADTs are, as the name suggests, a generalized form of algebraic data types. The name is a slight misnomer because they are really more of a generalized form of regular variant types only. *Algebraic data types* is a general name for both product and sum types taken together. Syntactically, GADTs look as follows:

```
/* src/Ch05/Ch05_GADTs.re */
type poNumber = string;

type paymentMethod =
| Cash: paymentMethod
| PurchaseOrder(poNumber): paymentMethod; /* (1) */

let paymentCash = Cash; /* (2) */

let paymentMessage(paymentMethod) = switch (paymentMethod) {
| Cash => "Paid in cash" /* (3) */
| PurchaseOrder(poNumber) => {j|Paid with PO#$poNumber|j}
};
```

1. GADT definition syntax looks much like regular variant definition syntax, except that the data constructors explicitly declare their type at the end. For monomorphic types (that is, ones that don't have any type parameters), this doesn't look very useful. In the next chapter, we'll see why it's so powerful.
2. Value construction looks the same as for regular variants.
3. Pattern matching also looks the same as for regular variants.

Designing for correctness with types

Now that we've seen the product and sum types in action, let's take a step back and ask how they can work together. Intuitively, product types let us group values together, and sum types let us choose one among a restricted set of values. Together, they express a wide range of data modeling scenarios. Let's look at a couple of examples.

Products and sums together

First, a simple example to warm up. Suppose we're asked to track the following attributes of a person for a Customer Relationship Management software:

- ID number: A string
- Name: A string
- Education level: *One of* school, college, postgrad, or other

A valid person record must have *all of* these attributes. Notice how we're using the specific phrasing *one of* and *all of*. These give us a hint about how to model the data: *one of* means a sum type and *all of* a product type! It's very useful to think about the requirements in these terms as we break down a data structure into its component parts.

The main choice after that is specifically which implementations of product and sum types to use. Usually, we'll reach for the simplest possible implementations: records and variants. So, in this case:

```
/* src/Ch05/Ch05_CrmPerson.re */
type education = Ch05_Variants.education =
| School
| College
| Postgrad
| Other;

type t = {id: int, name: string, education}; /* (1) */

/* (2) */
let bob = {id: 1, name: "Bob", education: College};
let jim = {id: 2, name: "Jim", education: Other};
```

1. The person record type Ch05_CrmPerson.t is a record type composed out of three other types: an int, a string, *and* an education. The education type is a variant type that admits *one of* the four legal education values.

2. The valid t values are built by grouping together all the required component values, including the education values.

Notice how the values are constructed by obeying the business logic laid out by the types: for a person record, we need an ID, a name, and an education; for an education value, we need only one of the allowable values.

Recursive types

Now, let's look at a more interesting example. Suppose we need to model not just one, but a *list* of person records. Suppose we also need to be able to walk through this list, one person at a time, and carry out some actions based on the data from each person. A natural data structure for this would be a *singly linked list.* As you might know, a singly linked list is a series of nodes that each point to the next node in the list, or to *nothing* in case there is no next node (that is, for the last node of the list).

In Reason, a natural way to model this list is with a recursive variant type. A *recursive type* is one that contains values of its *own* type. This neat trick works because Reason internally separates the storage of values from their types, so they don't end up taking infinite storage. Here's an example implementation of our person record list scenario:

```
/* src/Ch05/Ch05_PersonList.re */
type t = Node(Ch05_CrmPerson.t, t) | Empty; /* (1) */

let people = Ch05_CrmPerson.(Node(bob, Node(jim, Empty))); /* (2) */

let rec greet(t) = switch (t) { /* (3) */
| Node(person, list) => { /* (4) */
    print_endline("Hello, " ++ person.name ++ "!");
    greet(list)
  }
| Empty => () /* (5) */
};
```

Using a recursive type reveals some new and interesting syntax:

1. The type definition of a recursive type doesn't look any different from what we saw before, except that it contains a reference to its own type. We're not having to do anything special because, in Reason, all type definitions are recursive by default. In fact, if we want to make a type definition *non-recursive* (which we do in some circumstances), we'll need to use an extra keyword: type nonrec t = ...

2. We can define a value of a recursive type like normal, except it can contain other values of its own type. We locally open the `Ch05_CrmPerson` module to get access to the people values defined there.

3. To walk through all the values of a recursive type, we'll usually need a *recursive function* (that is, a function that calls itself). Unlike types, functions aren't recursive by default, because traditionally recursive functions are slightly more expensive in terms of runtime performance. So when we need recursion, we specify it with the `let rec ...` syntax.

4. We can destructure a recursive value in the normal way, just as if it were non-recursive; we just need to make sure we pass its recursive portion, `list`, into the recursive `greet` call.

5. To handle the non-recursive portion of `Ch05_PersonList.t` (`Empty`), we just need to *do nothing*, so we return unit, the *empty value*.

Our recursive `greet` function has an interesting property: it is tail-recursive. *Tail recursion* is the property that a recursive function has if it calls itself in tail position, that is, if it calls itself as the last (tail) operation of any of its branches of evaluation. For example, `greet` calls itself as the last operation of its first branch, where it handles the `Node` variant case.

We're paying attention to this tail recursion property because the BuckleScript compiler has a special ability to convert tail recursion into a simple, efficient loop in the output JavaScript. If you examine the output, you'll see that the loop looks almost handwritten.

Summary

In this chapter, we covered what collectively are known as sum types: variants and pattern matching, polymorphic variants, and GADTs. These are some of the bread-and-butter typing techniques in Reason, and they enable powerful data modeling techniques when used in the right combinations.

However, it's becoming increasingly clear that a lot of typing power still remains to be explored. In the next chapter, we will fully cover the type parameters (generics) that we've glimpsed at so far while using different kinds of type techniques.

6
Making Types That Can Slot into Any Other Type

In the previous chapter, we saw how to express types for values that have the potential to be one of several different things at runtime. At certain times in the last chapter, and throughout the book so far, we came up against types that Reason marked as *to be filled in later*. In this chapter, we will cover these types more in more detail, specifically the following topics:

- Reason's generic type inference
- What are type parameters?
- Common parameterized types such as lists, options, and arrays
- Adding parameters to sum and product types
- Type inference restrictions on parameterized mutable types

Type inference and generic types

Let's look at a few interesting examples of Reason's type inference and how it decides what types need to be *filled in later*, as illustrated in the following snippet:

```
/* src/Ch06/Ch06_GenericInference.re */
let triple(x) = (x, x, x); /* (1) */
let wrap(x) = `wrap(x); /* (2) */
let makeObj(x) = {as _; pub x = x}; /* (3) */
let greet(x) = print_endline({j|Hello, $x!|j}); /* (4) */
```

These examples all have something in common: the compiler doesn't have quite enough information to infer their *concrete* types. Instead, it infers what it can about their general shape but leaves some parts as *generic*. We can observe the following:

1. In (1), the type is inferred as `'a => ('a, 'a, 'a)`.
2. In (2), the type is inferred as `'a => [> `wrap('a)]`.
3. In (3), the type is inferred as `'a => {. x: 'a}`.
4. In (4), the type is inferred as `'a => unit`.

In each of these cases, the compiler infers some of the types as `'a`, or in other words, *I don't know yet*. Let's look at the first case, the `triple` function, to try to understand why.

In `triple`, the function parameter is x and the function body is `(x, x, x)`. Given these two facts, the compiler tries to infer (that is, narrow down) the type of `triple` by working its way up from each part of the function parameter and body. Let's look at what we can infer from each part of `triple`:

- From the x parameter: Nothing, so we mark its type as (a generic type) `'a`
- From the body, `(x, x, x)`: We already marked the type of x as `'a`, so we mark the type of the body as `('a, 'a, 'a)`, that is, a tuple type consisting of three elements all of the same type
- From the overall function: We marked the parameter as type `'a`, and the body as type `('a, 'a, 'a)`, so we infer the function as a whole to have type `'a => ('a, 'a, 'a)`

Notice that, if anything, this seems like a process of elimination, or a process of solving a Sudoku puzzle. We narrow down the types as much as we can based on what we know until we can't narrow them down any further. This is the same inference and unification process we're familiar with from previous chapters where we encountered various type errors, but with generic types we see a new dimension to the type system.

 Reason's type inference process is a famous one, known as **Hindley-Milner (H-M)** type inference; it's a mathematics-specific way of examining any given expression to try to deduce the most general type that will fit the expression. We won't delve into the theory here, but we will cover the practicalities of working with H-M type inference.

By examining the type inference process for `triple`, we can see how the inference works for `wrap`, `makeObj`, and `greet`. The key point to understand is that each of these functions has a body expression that doesn't use any specific property of its input parameter; instead, the body composes the input parameter inside a larger expression that uses the value in a generic way that doesn't expose any information about the type itself. For example, imagine being given some object (you don't know what) and immediately putting it inside a box; you still don't know what the object is, you just know you now have a box that contains some object. This is how generic type inference works for structural types.

The special case of interpolation

Out of the functions we've mentioned, `greet` is a bit special because type inference doesn't work in quite the same way as it does for the others. For the first three functions, inference arrives at a generic type because the parameters are used in structurally-typed expressions. For `greet` though, the x parameter is interpolated into a string; however, strings aren't structurally typed! What's going on is that string interpolation is a special escape hatch provided by the BuckleScript compiler that allows you to turn any value into a string, but only when targeting JavaScript.

The key point here is turning any value into a string. We can think of this behavior as a function, `'a => string`. Since we then print the string with `print_endline`, the final result type is `unit`; so the overall type is `'a => unit`.

Type parameters

We've seen that type checking goes through an algorithmic process of working out the most general possible type of any given expression, and when the expression is structurally typed, such as `let pair(x) = (x, x)`, it can infer types that are parameterized (such as `'a => ('a, 'a)`) because it doesn't know, or doesn't need to know, exactly what they are.

A **type parameter** is an as-yet-unknown type that will be specified later in use. Reason supports type parameters on all types, including nominal types. This gives record and variant types a new dimension (literally) of data modeling power. Let's now explore a few of the most basic but also important parameterized data types in Reason.

The list – modeling more than one

We've already seen how to model a list of person records in Chapter 5, *Putting Alternative Values in Types,* but that data structure was limited to holding only values of person records. Ideally, we want a data structure that can hold values of *any* type, so that we don't have to re-implement the type and its operations for every possible element type. We can accomplish this by parameterizing the list type by the element type, as follows:

```
/* src/Ch06/Ch06_List.re */
type list('a) = Cons('a, list('a)) | Empty; /* (1) */

/* (2) */
let people = Ch04_RecordLiterals.(Cons(bob, Cons(jim, Cons(tom, Empty))));

/* (3) */
let greetOne({Ch04_RecordLiterals.id, name}) = print_endline(
  {j|Hello, $name with ID $id!|j});

let rec greetAll(people) = switch (people) {
| Cons(person, people) => { /* (4) */
  greetOne(person);
  greetAll(people)
  }
| Empty => () /* (5) */
};
```

The previous example shows how to generically hold objects of any given type, as well as do something specific with them. It is explained as follows:

1. Here, we parameterize a nominal type (a variant type to be precise), list, with an explicit type parameter, 'a (pronounced 'alpha'). Here we have only one, but types can have multiple type parameters. The syntax for declaring type parameters is type typeName('param1, 'param2, ..., 'paramN). Note that type parameters must always start with the tick (') character to distinguish them from regular types. Type parameters are also known as type variables.

2. We construct a list made up of person records we defined in a previous module. The compiler can infer its type to be list(Ch04_RecordLiterals.person), because we slotted in the person type at the exact places where we declared the type parameter, 'a.

3. We define how to greet a single person. This operation doesn't make use of type parameters in any way, but it is a building block for a later operation that does.

4. Inside `greetAll`, we have an interesting pattern match on `people`. With the `Cons(person, people)` and `Empty` branches, the compiler infers that `people` has type `list('a)`, and with `greetOne(person)`, it infers that `'a = person`; overall the function has the type `list(person) => unit`.

5. When we reach the end of the list, we don't want to do anything else, so we just return `()`.

Now that we've seen how to build and operate on a polymorphic data type, let's look at Reason's built-in implementation of the `list` type. The built-in implementation works in much the same way as the one mentioned earlier, except Reason provides some nice syntactic sugar to make it easier to work with lists. Let's take a look at the following snippet:

```
/* src/Ch06/Ch06_ReasonList.re */
let people = Ch04_RecordLiterals.[bob, jim, tom]; /* (1) */

let rec greetAll(people) = switch (people) {
| [person, ...people] => { /* (2) */
    Ch06_List.greetOne(person); /* (3) */
    greetAll(people)
  }
| [] => () /* (4) */
};
```

First of all, notice that we got rid of the type declaration, since the Reason `list('a)` type is already built in and accessible from every module. To be precise, it's defined in the `Pervasives` module, whose contents are by default accessible from every module.

1. We use the list construction syntactic sugar, which is `[elem1, elem2, ... elemN]`, to construct a list that is essentially like our previous one `Cons(elem1, Cons(elem2, ... Cons(elemN, Empty) ... ))`. The brackets-and-commas syntax is flatter and easier to understand.

2. Pattern matching on a list now looks like `[elem, ...restElems]` to bind to the first element and the list of remaining elements. The `...` is called the **spread operator** and is designed to look like JavaScript's array spread feature, which works similarly.

3. We reuse the `greetOne` function we already defined since it doesn't depend on the specific list type—it just greets a single person.

4. The empty list pattern now looks like `[]` instead of `Empty`.

Notice how succinct the list syntax is overall. It's designed for everyday use because lists are one of the most important data types in Reason, and in functional programming in general.

The option – modeling either none or one

In a similar way to `list('a)`, the `Pervasives` module also provides a data type, `option('a)`. This time let's look at its real definition, because there's no syntactic sugar for it, as follows:

```
type option('a) = Some('a) | None;
```

In some ways, this is a simpler data type than the list. Its real utility comes from the meaning we give to the variant cases:

- `Some('a)`: Represents a value that is present and that is known
- `None`: Represents a value that is absent and is unknown

In Reason, and some other languages, there is no concept of a null value, so this option type is used to represent that a value is present or absent. Whenever we'd use null, we can use options instead, with the benefit that optionality (the property that some value may be present or not) is captured in the type system, instead of behind the scenes. Because the `option` type is a variant, the compiler helps us to handle possible missing values through exhaustivity checking. There's no danger of forgetting to handle a null value and crashing at runtime.

Present and absent may still be somewhat vague concepts, so the following code is a more concrete example where we try to find a matching value in a list:

```
/* src/Ch06/Ch06_Option.re */
let rec tryFind(needle, haystack) = switch (haystack) { /* (1) */
| [item, ..._items] when needle(item) => Some(item) /* (2) */
| [_item, ...items] => tryFind(needle, items) /* (3) */
| [] => None /* (4) */
};

let optionallyGreet(person) = switch (person) { /* (5) */
| Some(person) => Ch06_List.greetOne(person)
| None => print_endline("No such person!")
};

let idEq1({Ch04_RecordLiterals.id}) = id == 1; /* (6) */
```

```
let idEq4({Ch04_RecordLiterals.id}) = id == 4;

optionallyGreet(tryFind(idEq1, Ch06_ReasonList.people)); /* (7) */
optionallyGreet(tryFind(idEq4, Ch06_ReasonList.people));
```

In this example, we define how to find an item in a list and safely handle the case of a missing item:

1. We pass in a list to search (called `haystack`) and a tester function (called `needle`) that tells us if we've found the value we're looking for. Since `haystack` is a list, we can pattern match on it.

2. The first pattern looks at the first element of the list to see if it's the one we want, as determined by `needle`. We don't want to bind the rest of the elements, so we prefix the `_items` name with an underscore to tell Reason to ignore it. Notice that we're using the `when` clause here, as introduced in `Chapter 5`, *Putting Alternative Values in Types*. This is equivalent to using an `if` expression inside the body of the branch, but is slightly more succinct. If the first element matches the needle, we put it inside a `Some` constructor and evaluate it.

3. In the second pattern, we match against the remaining list of items after ignoring the first item, and recursively try to find the element we want in that. But this branch is only reached if the first branch doesn't match, meaning that the element wasn't the first item in the list. The branch itself evaluates to the result of `tryFind`, meaning either `Some(person)` or `None`.

4. In the final branch, we must handle the other possible state of the `haystack` list: being empty. If it is, we either started with an empty list or ended up with one by recursion. In either case, we didn't find the element we wanted in the list, so we return `None`, which in this case means not found.

5. Here, we describe how to greet a person who may or may not be there. The compiler forces handling both `Some(person)` and `None` cases—we can't forget to handle a missing value.

6. We define two different `needle` functions, which test whether a given person's record has the ID 1 or 4.

7. Here's the payoff: we can optionally greet a person, but only if we found the person with the given ID in our `people` list. We can run the following output script to see what happens:

```
$ node src/Ch06/Ch06_Option.bs.js
Hello, Bob with ID 1!
No such person!
```

As expected, we find and greet the person (Bob) with ID 1, but not the one with ID 4 because there is no such person.

 In the output JavaScript, BuckleScript again converts the tail-recursive tryFind function into a simple imperative loop.

Here, we see two sides of using the option type: we may need to represent the presence or absence of a value during the normal course of our operation, and if we use a variant type such as option, we get the benefit of its exhaustivity checking.

Mutable parameterized types – ref and array

Reason also provides two important parameterized types that allow their values to be mutated in place. This mutability brings efficiency gains for certain types of algorithms, but generally needs to be used carefully because, as we'll see, it may be a source of bugs.

Managing a reference to a value

We've already seen an example of mutability, in the *Mutable record fields* section of Chapter 4, *Grouping Values Together in Types*. Sometimes, we need to manage just one or two mutable values, and we might not want to go through the ceremony of declaring a new record type with mutable fields. For these situations, we can take advantage of the built-in ref type. The ref type essentially gives us a box, a ref, that lets us swap values in and out. The values themselves need not be mutable, just the box itself:

```
type ref('a) = {mutable contents: 'a}; /* (1) */
let ref: 'a => ref('a); /* (2) */
let (:=): (ref('a), 'a) => unit; /* (3) */
let (^): ref('a) => 'a; /* (4) */
let incr: ref(int) => unit; /* (5) */
let decr: ref(int) => unit;
```

The previous code listing shows the complete API of the ref type, explained as follows:

1. It's implemented as a record type with just a single mutable record field, but this field is parameterized by a type parameter, 'a, letting us reuse it for any type.
2. We can use the ref function to box a value of any type and put it inside a ref:
   let count = ref(0);.

3. The assignment operator (:=) is implemented as a function and can be used in the infix position: `count := 1;`.

4. The dereference operator, (^), is also implemented as a function, but Reason allows us to use it in postfix position: `let countVal = count^;`.

5. `incr` and `decr` are convenience functions for incrementing and decrementing integers, as we often need to update counts.

The huge benefit of using the `ref` type to manage mutation is that mutability is captured at the type level. We can tell from looking at any type signature that contains `ref(something)` that something of the `something` type is changing. By contrast, when we're using a mutable record field directly, we have no type-level indication of mutability, just the record definition itself.

Let's look at an example of using a `ref`: redefining the `tryGreet` function to use a more imperative style of walking through its input list and trying to find the required item. We'll need three refs: the remaining portion of the haystack list, whether we should stop searching or not, and an optional found item. As long as we haven't found the item yet, we'll keep searching, but as soon as we find it, we'll return it:

```reason
/* src/Ch06/Ch06_Ref.re */
let tryFind(needle, haystack) = {
  let currHaystack = ref(haystack);
  let stop = ref(false);
  let currItem = ref(None);

  while (!(stop^)) { /* (1) */
    switch (currHaystack^) { /* (2) */
    | [item, ..._items] when needle(item) => { /* (3) */
        stop := true;
        currItem := Some(item)
      }
    | [_item, ...items] => currHaystack := items /* (4) */
    | [] => stop := true /* (5) */
    };
  };

  currItem^ /* (6) */
};
```

In the previous example, we use Reason's imperative features (mutation and looping), explained as follows:

1. We continuously loop until we explicitly say we should stop. Notice that an imperative `while` loop looks exactly as we might expect from other imperative languages such as JavaScript.
2. Pattern matching on the input `haystack list` is still the most convenient way to walk through it item by item, so we keep doing that here.
3. If we find the item we're looking for, we need to make sure that we set the stop indicator to `true`, and also set the found item so we can return it later.
4. If we haven't found it yet but the list isn't empty, set the current haystack to be the remainder of the list.
5. If the list is empty, we obviously haven't found the item, so we need to stop.
6. Whatever we've found (or haven't) so far, we finally need to dereference and return it.

The first thing to notice about this imperative version is that it's more verbose. Keeping track of the mutable state involves some ceremony at the code level. It's not that imperative style in Reason is especially cumbersome; it would look much the same in any imperative language. It's just that functional style with recursion is, in general, more succinct because the recursive call effectively keeps track of the current state so we don't have to.

The second thing to note is that we've preserved the same function signature (`('a => bool, list('a)) => option('a)`) for this implementation, just without recursion. If we needed to, we could swap out this implementation for the recursive one, and our client code wouldn't need a recompilation to use it. This is a property of many static type systems: if we preserve type signatures, we can freely swap out implementations. Reason's type system in particular uses signatures to decide whether entire modules are compatible. This helps us pinpoint compatibility issues early, at build time, rather than find an incompatibility when running the code.

Managing an array of values

Sometimes, we need to efficiently manage and change many values of the same type. Reason provides the `array` type to help with this. We can think of an array as a single contiguous line of boxes of the same size, each of which can hold a value of the same type. Formally, it's a polymorphic type, as follows:

```
type array('a);
```

The `array` data structure is characteristically similar to what you might have seen in other languages, in which:

- It allows random access to its elements
- It doesn't allow recursive traversal of elements like `list` does with the spread (`[item, ...items]`) operation

However, it does allow basic pattern matching on its elements. The following is an example of its use:

```
/* src/Ch06/Ch06_Array.re */
let empty = [||]; /* (1) */
let singleton = [|1|];
let multi = [|false, true, true|];

multi[1] = false; /* (2) */
Js.log(multi[1]); /* (3) */
```

In the previous example, we see the following simple use of arrays:

1. We can create an empty array, as well as arrays with one or more elements. The array delimiters are `[|` and `|]` and are used to distinguish them from lists which are more frequently used in Reason.
2. We can assign to any valid index in the array (assigning to an out-of-bounds index will cause a runtime exception).
3. We can read the value at any valid index (reading from an out-of-bounds index will also cause a runtime exception).

For arrays, the concept of indexing is important, as we can see here. Index-based random access is constant-time, but in return we have to take care to access only valid indexes.

To get a better sense of how arrays are useful, let's try to implement a tic-tac-toe board using an array and a couple of functions that update and check the board, as follows:

```
/* src/Ch06/Ch06_TicTacToe.re */

/* Each slot on the board can be taken by X or O, or it can be empty. */
type slot = X | O | Empty;

let newBoard() = Array.make(9, Empty); /* (1) */

/* Coords are as follows on the board:
   1 2 3
   4 5 6
   7 8 9 */
```

```reason
let play(player, coord, board) = board[coord - 1] = player; /* (2) */

let xWon(board) = switch (board) {
| [|X, X, X, /* (3) */
    _, _, _,
    _, _, _|]
| [|_, _, _, /* (4) */
    X, X, X,
    _, _, _|]
| [|_, _, _,
    _, _, _,
    X, X, X|]
| [|X, _, _,
    X, _, _,
    X, _, _|]
| [|_, X, _,
    _, X, _,
    _, X, _|]
| [|_, _, X,
    _, _, X,
    _, _, X|]
| [|X, _, _,
    _, X, _,
    _, _, X|]
| [|_, _, X,
    _, X, _,
    X, _, _|] => true /* (5) */
| _ => false /* (6) */
};
```

This is an interesting example of designing an array so we can pattern match it literally, explained as follows:

1. We can create a new game board by creating a new array filled with Empty slots, using the Array.make library function. This function gives us an array of the required length and is filled with a single value in all the indexes.
2. Since we accept a one-indexed board coordinate, we convert it to a zero-indexed array index by simply subtracting one.
3. We can pattern match against the exact structure of the array. In this case, our nine-element array can look exactly like a tic-tac-toe board if we break it up into three rows purely for presentation.
4. We can use or patterns to capture all the cases in which player X wins.
5. Return true for all of them.
6. Otherwise, we return false.

In this case, the fact that we can easily set any position on the board when a player makes a move suits the random-access capability of an array. Setting random positions in a list would be an inefficient operation by comparison because the only way to do that is to traverse each element of the list and then perform several list-breaking and joining operations until we create the final output list.

In general, an array is very useful when we need to perform frequent updates over multiple elements. Common scenarios are pixel buffers and manually managed memory regions. Fortunately, Reason makes these scenarios relatively easy to implement.

Mutation and type inference restrictions

In general, the compiler happily infers all sorts of types for us, but it does have some limitations. Sometimes, we need to give it a little nudge to help it get to the correct inference result, for example. The main case we need to be aware of is called **value restriction.** Value restriction basically means that mutable values can't be generic, the compiler must know their types fully. The following is an example error you will get if you uncomment the code in the file src/Ch06/Ch06_ValueRestrictionError.re:

```
(Output from bsb -w)
  We've found a bug for you!
  src/Ch06/Ch06_ValueRestrictionError.re 2:17-24
  1 | /* src/Ch06/Ch06_ValueRestrictionError.re */
  2 | let optionArr = [|None|];
  3 | let optionRef = ref(None);
  This expression's type contains type variables that can't be generalized:
  array(option('_a))
  This happens when the type system senses there's a mutation/side-effect,
in combination with a polymorphic value.
  Using or annotating that value usually solves it. More info:
  https://realworldocaml.org/v1/en/html/imperative-programming-1.html#side-ef
fects-and-weak-polymorphism
```

Notice the inferred type for optionArr: array(option('_a)). The underscore prefix in front of the type variable name is the compiler's way of saying that it ran into the value restriction. A type variable named '_a is called a **weak type variable** (in the sense that its actual type might change later).

Having a type that might change after it's inferred at compilation is a bad idea. For example, let's think about what would happen if the compiler inferred the type as `array(option('a))`. Later in the code, we could set that index to `Some(1)`, then later still we could set it to `Some(false)`. This would defeat the type system entirely and leave us uncertain of what the exact type is at any point in the code. The compiler designers decided to prevent this from happening. This is just one of the type soundness decisions that they've made over the years to prevent runtime type errors from creeping into programs.

As a valid code, we could precise the type using `array(option(string))`, as you can see in the alternative code file (`src/Ch06/Ch06_ValueRestrictionErrorFixed.re`) which compiles correctly. It's code is as follows:

```
/* src/Ch06/Ch06_ValueRestrictionErrorFixed.re */
let optionArr: array(option(string)) = [|None|];
let optionRef: ref(option(string)) = ref(None);
```

Let's look at another value restriction error. Again, uncomment the code in the file `src/Ch06/Ch06_ValueRestrictionOtherError.re`, and you will get a compilation error as follows:

```
(Output from bsb -w)
We've found a bug for you!
  src/Ch06/Ch06_ValueRestrictionOtherError.re 5:15-28
  1 | /* src/Ch06/Ch06_ValueRestrictionOtherError.re */
  2 | let pair(x) = (x, x);
  3 | let pairAll = List.map(pair);
  This expression's type contains type variables that can't be generalized:
  list('_a) => list(('_a, '_a))
  This happens when the type system senses there's a mutation/side-effect,
in combination with a polymorphic value.
  Using or annotating that value usually solves it. More info:
  https://realworldocaml.org/v1/en/html/imperative-programming-1.html#side-ef
  fects-and-weak-polymorphism
```

This one is slightly trickier as there's no obvious mutation. The `pairAll` function is supposed to convert a list of items into a list of pairs (2-tuples) of those items. The problem is that the `pair` function is generic; the compiler can't figure out if it might be mutating anything. If we'd had a monomorphic (that is, not generic) function instead, such as `let pair(x) = (x + 1, x - 1);`, then the compiler would be able to figure out that the inputs and outputs are just `int` and there's no mutation involved.

However, there is another way to solve this particular error; remember that it's called the *value* restriction. In other words, only values are restricted like this. If we expand `pairAll` into an explicit function, then the error goes away, shown as follows:

```
let pairAll(list) = List.map(pair, list);
```

Our fixed code can be found in `src/Ch06/Ch06_ValueRestrictionErrorFixed.re`.

This funny solution convinces the compiler that yes, this is really a function, so the value restriction doesn't apply.

Forcing a difference with phantom types

Because we can declare types that can slot in *any* type parameters, that includes type parameters that the types don't actually use. These are called phantom type parameters, or more informally **phantom types.**

A common use case for phantom types is in a kind of type-safe **builder pattern.** (The builder pattern is a piece of code that helps us to construct an object according to specific rules.) For example, we might want to construct syntactically valid SQL statements. One way to do that is to have a validator function that takes an input SQL statement and decides whether it follows SQL syntax rules or not at runtime. This function might try to parse the input statement and build an expression tree. If the tree can be built, the statement is valid. Otherwise, it's invalid.

Another way to approach this is to provide a set of functions that statically enforce that only syntactically valid statements can be created. The magic part of this is that we can tell the compiler exactly what the type parameter should be when it's not actually used in the type body. There's nothing in the type definition to contradict what we say, so the compiler must accept it.

The following is a simplified example:

```
/* src/Ch06/Ch06_PhantomTypes.re */

module Sql: {
  type column = string; /* (1) */
  type table = string;
  type t('a); /* (2) */

  let select: list(column) => t([`select]); /* (3) */
  let from: (table, t([`select])) => t([`ok]);
  let print: t([`ok]) => string;
```

```
} = {
  type column = string;
  type table = string;
  type t('a) = string;

  let select(columns) = { /* (4) */
    let commalist = String.concat(", ", columns);
    {j|select $commalist|j}
  };

  let from(table, t) = {j|$t from $table|j};
  let print(t) = t; /* (5) */
};

let sql = Sql.(select(["name"]) |> from("employees") |> print); /* (6) */
Js.log(sql);
```

For the sake of simplicity, we're dealing with only the `select` and `from` clauses in this SQL builder module, explained as follows:

1. We alias a couple of types to serve as documentation.
2. This is the type with the phantom type parameter; to the module consumer, it looks like a normal parameterized type. Internally, it doesn't contain, or otherwise use, any values of its parameter type.
3. This function is the entry point into the build: it takes a column list and returns a partially constructed SQL statement. We can't do anything with this returned value except feed it into the next function, `from`. Notice that the type parameters are literally the types of polymorphic variants named appropriately; they just act as tags.
4. The implementations of `select` and `from` are very simple: they just build normal strings in the form of syntactically valid SQL statements. The most interesting thing about them is that their types are enforced to take parameters such that they can only be called in a particular order: `select, from, print`.
5. The `print` function is strikingly simple in that it just returns the built string. We can examine that and then pass it into an SQL engine to run.
6. We build a syntactically valid SQL statement by calling the functions in the right order, enforced by the type system, and we then output them to the terminal. Note that the `|>` operator is called **pipe-forward**, and it's used to feed the output of one function as the input of the next one. We'll cover common operators in the next chapter.

The following code is the error we would have gotten if we'd tried to print an invalid SQL statement:

```
(Output from bsb -w)
We've found a bug for you!
  src/Ch06/Ch06_PhantomTypes.re 25:36-40
  23 | };
  24 |
  25 | let sql = Sql.(select(["name"]) |> print); /* (6) */
  26 | Js.log(sql);
  This has type:
    Sql.t([ `ok ]) => string
  But somewhere wanted:
    Sql.t([ `select ]) => 'a
  These two variant types have no intersection
```

This type error is saying that the `print` function expects a complete `ok` SQL statement, but has received only a `select` clause. The type parameters, working together with the module's functions, ensure that the SQL is constructed in the right way.

Summary

In this chapter, we delved into Reason's parameterized types, learning about type parameters and how they expand types to become generic, some common parameterized types that we use in Reason, the compiler's restrictions on using parameterized types and mutation together, and how to force the same underlying type to look different to the compiler using phantom type parameters.

We also saw some instances of passing in functions as arguments to other functions, for example, `tryFind` and `List.map`. In the next chapter, we'll thoroughly cover functions and how Reason lets us treat them as first-class objects that we can pass around to allow our code to behave flexibly.

Summary

7
Making Types That Represent Operations

In previous chapters, we've seen how to build types to model many kinds of data. Through all of these chapters, we've relied on functions. Functions wrap calculations and actions for easy reuse, so it makes sense that they're among the most heavily used features in any programming language. So, by taking advantage of Reason's type system and functional programming techniques, we can design functions for maximum effectiveness.

In this chapter, we will cover the following topics:

- Meaningful function types and useful properties
- Currying and partial application
- Higher-order functions
- Using functions to control dependency ordering and program flow
- Commonly used functions and operators

But first, what is a function? A **function** in type theory and mathematics has a formal definition, but we can think of it as a formula for calculating an output given an input. In Reason and other statically-typed functional programming languages, functions *always* have an output, even if they don't actually calculate anything. We'll examine how to express these inputs and outputs, but we first need a basic understanding of function types and properties.

Function types and other useful properties

In Reason, functions have very specific types and, just like other values, functions of different types can't be substituted for one another.

The basic type of every Reason function is as follows:

```
a => b
```

Read this as *a arrow b*.

As you can see, the input, a, and the output, b, can be any type (even the same one). This basic function type, with a single input and a single output, gives rise to every other function type in Reason. We'll cover how this happens shortly, but first let's talk about a couple of useful functional programming concepts that are important in the type-driven world.

Referential transparency

The first property, called **referential transparency** (or **RT**), means that a function will always produce the same output, b, for a given input, a, no matter how, when, or how many times we call it. This means that a function can't behave unpredictably; we must be able to predict its output for every input, purely like a mathematical formula.

For example, the following is a non-referentially transparent function:

```
/* [xDaysAgo(x)] returns the time [x] days before now, in ms since Unix
     epoch. */
let xDaysAgo(x) =
  Js.Date.now() -. float_of_int(x) *. 24. *. 60. *. 60. *. 1_000.;
```

 In Reason, float arithmetic operators are distinct from integer operators (they are suffixed with a dot). Reason tries to be as explicit as possible about arithmetic and conversions so that we can avoid surprising results.

We can't tell what the output will be for any given input, x, because that depends on the date and time the function is called. The problem instead is the hidden dependency on the current date or time. One solution is to remove the dependency by passing it in as a function argument, as follows:

```
/* [xDaysAgo(now, x)] returns the time [x] days before [now], in ms
     since Unix epoch. */
let xDaysAgo(now, x) =
  now -. float_of_int(x) *. 24. *. 60. *. 60. *. 1_000.;
```

The immediate benefit is that the function is easier to test, but the bigger benefit is that functions such as this in the codebase make it easier to reason about.

Reasoning about code (also known as **equational reasoning**) means being able to substitute actual values in place of function arguments, and just like a math equation, evaluate to the result by simplifying it. This sounds like a trivial benefit, but when used over a codebase, it can be a powerful technique for ensuring transparency.

Realistically speaking, we can't make the entire codebase referentially transparent (unless we use advanced techniques such as effect types). We can, however, push out the non-RT operations to the edges of the program. For example, we can call the (second) xDaysAgo function with either the result of a call to Js.Date.now() or a date value passed in from somewhere else. This is a simple but effective form of **dependency injection** (passing in values to a program instead of letting the program try to get the values itself). We'll cover dependency injection in more detail later on in this chapter.

Function purity

The second important property that we try to achieve is **purity**. This concept means that, to the caller (that is, the code that calls it) and the outside world, a function has no impact other than evaluating to its result. We say that the function does not have any **observable effects**. Observability is the crucial thing here; there may well be effects happening and contained inside the function (such as mutation), but the caller doesn't, and cannot, know about them. The following is an example of a pure function that mutates internally but not observably:

```
let sum(numbers) = {
  let result = ref(0);
  for (i in 0 to Array.length(numbers) - 1) {
    result := result^ + numbers[i];
  };
  result^
};
```

If we were to add a Js.log(result^) inside the body of the for loop, the function would become impure because its effects would become observable. People sometimes disagree with what exactly observable means, especially in the context of logging the operations of otherwise-pure functions, but it's safe to err on the side of caution and accept that any observable effect is an impurity in the function (and that's OK, because sometimes we actually need those observable effects).

Totality

The last important property that we want functions to have is **totality**. This means that functions should handle every possible value of the type that they accept, which is actually trickier than it seems! For example, look at the xDaysAgo function again. What happens if x is negative? Or very large or small? Did we account for integer overflow? Especially when working with numbers, we need to understand their properties on the platform we're running on top of.

In our case, we're running on a JavaScript platform such as Node.js, so all numbers are internally represented as IEEE floats (that's how JavaScript works) and we can get pretty far before we need to worry about overflow. But consider the following trivial function:

```
let sendMoney(from: string, to_: string, amount: float) = Js.log(
  {j|Send \$$amount from $from to $to_|j});
```

 The first dollar symbol needs to be escaped, otherwise the compiler tries to treat it as starting an interpolation.

Here, we're just printing out what we want to happen. In a real application, we might want to do a money transfer. Suppose we exposed this function with an HTTP service call. What would happen if someone called the service with a negative float? The best-case scenario is that the error would be caught somewhere else; the worst is that people could make calls to siphon money out of other people's accounts.

One approach to solving this is to validate our arguments at the very beginning of the function, as follows:

```
let sendMoney(from, to_, amount) = {
  assert(from != "");
  assert(to_ != "");
  assert(amount > 0.);
  Js.log({j|Send \$$amount from $from to $to_|j});
};
```

For good measure, in this snippet, we're doing some basic validation on the sender and receiver strings. We're also able to get rid of the type annotations because the assertions will cause them to be inferred correctly.

assert is a built-in keyword, although it looks and works like a function.

From the function's point of view, internally it's now a total function because it explicitly errors on the cases it doesn't want to handle, but does handle the remaining happy path. To the outside world, however, the function is still taking in raw strings and floats, and failing to handle most of them. A better solution is to use more constrained types to describe exactly what the function can accept, as follows:

```
/* src/Ch07/Ch07_DomainTypes.re */
module NonEmptyString: { /* (1) */
  type t = pri string; /* (2) */
  let makeExn: string => t;
} = {
  type t = string;
  let makeExn(string) = { assert(string != ""); string };
};

module PositiveFloat: { /* (3) */
  type t = pri float;
  let makeExn: float => t;
} = {
  type t = float;
  let makeExn(float) = { assert(float > 0.); float };
  let toFloat(t) = t;
};

let sendMoney( /* (4) */
  from: NonEmptyString.t,
  to_: NonEmptyString.t,
  amount: PositiveFloat.t) = {

  let from = (from :> string); /* (5) */
  let to_ = (to_ :> string);
  let amount = (amount :> float);
  Js.log({j|Send \$$amount from $from to $to_|j});
};

sendMoney( /* (6) */
  NonEmptyString.makeExn("Alice"),
  NonEmptyString.makeExn("Bob"),
  PositiveFloat.makeExn(32.));
```

We had to use `to_` as the parameter name instead of `to` because the latter is a reserved keyword in Reason. It's a common practice to add an underscore to a keyword if we want to use it as a name.

This snippet looks more verbose, but in the long run is the better solution because we can write tests for the wrapper types and their modules in isolation, get peace of mind that the types really do enforce our rules, and reuse the types instead of adding checks throughout the codebase. Here's how it works:

1. We set up a type whose values can only be non-empty strings. If a caller tries to construct an empty string of the type, that will fail with an exception.
2. The type declaration says that this is a `private` type, meaning that we expose its internal representation, but we don't allow users to construct values of the type. This is a useful technique when we want to semi-transparently take an existing type and restrict it in some way. We will see how to do that shortly.
3. Similarly, we set up a type whose values can be only positive floats.
4. In the `sendMoney` function, we reap the benefit of these types by only accepting these constrained types instead of their raw variants. The function is now total because it only accepts exactly the values it works with by (type) definition.
5. We still need to unwrap the constrained values to get at the raw ones, because ultimately we want to print the raw values. Because the types are declared as `private` though, we can **coerce** them back to their more general versions. Coercion means forcing a value of a constrained type (such as `NonEmptyString.t`) back to being a more general type (such as `string`). Coercion is completely static; if we can't coerce something, we'll get a compile error. Note that the syntax for coercion needs to be pretty exact, and it needs to include the parentheses.
6. We also need to wrap the values before we pass them into the function. This is the point that can potentially fail, so we've moved it outside of our function implementation.

Here, we've used the convention of adding `Exn` to the names of the functions that may throw exceptions. Some people prefer to return optional values instead of throwing exceptions. This convention is idiomatic and type-safe, but is ultimately just another method of reporting errors. The key point to take away is that any possible failures have been moved out of our total `sendMoney` function, and other functions that use constrained types.

What a function type means

In the context of type-driven development, why are functional programming concepts such as referential transparency, purity, and totality important? The reason is that a function's type has a well-understood mathematical meaning, and breaking such rules muddy this meaning.

A function type such as a => b means that a function of this type will accept an input of type a and evaluate to a result of type b, and will do nothing else (for example, print out a log, start the coffee maker, or launch missiles). We like having this guarantee in much the same way that we like knowing that an int is just an int, and not a missile launch followed by an int.

The fact that Reason allows side effects is a great pragmatic decision, but we can still strive to push the side effects to the very edges of our programs and keep their cores purely functional. Purity in the functional sense is necessary for the type of a function to be accurate. If types in our program are accurate, we can perform type-driven development with more confidence.

Multiple arguments and currying

We've already mentioned that Reason functions always accept a single argument and return a single value, but we've been happily using functions that look like they take multiple arguments, for example, xDaysAgo(now, x). How is this possible?

In Reason, functions with multiple arguments are automatically **curried**. This means that they are actually functions that accept a single argument and return a new function, which accepts the next argument, and so on, forming a chain of single-argument functions that finally return a result. This might seem like it's inefficient, but in practice the compiler can almost always optimize the chain of calls into a single, efficient call. Let's look at the following concrete example, defining xDaysAgo:

```
let xDaysAgo(now, x) = ...;
```

This syntax is equivalent to the following (which is supported by the Reason code formatter tool, and thus usually seen in the wild):

```
let xDaysAgo = (now, x) => ...;
```

Next, we have the following:

```
let xDaysAgo = now => x => ...;
```

Similarly, we can call the following function:

```
let result = xDaysAgo(now, x);
```

That is equivalent to the following syntax:

```
let result = xDaysAgo(now)(x);
```

The compiler understands that this syntax is a **fully applied** function call, and optimizes accordingly.

Sometimes, a call isn't fully applied. In other words, it's **partially applied**. This means that it has been called with only some of the arguments that it accepts. A partially-applied function is just a function that accepts one or more arguments but, by definition, fewer arguments than the original function. Let's look at the following simple example:

```
let xDaysBeforeNow = xDaysAgo(Js.Date.now());
let result = xDaysBeforeNow(10);
```

This example captures the current moment in time by making a call to the appropriate JavaScript date function and then feeds or injects it into the xDaysAgo function to get back a new function that's been primed with the current time. This new function is then bound to the name xDaysBeforeNow and called to get a result. The result will be deterministic; in other words, we'll always get back the same output for a given input. The reason is that the non-deterministic data has already been *fed* into the function and is captured as a static value inside it. In other words, xDaysBeforeNow is also referentially transparent.

As a rule, functions that we get from applications of a referentially-transparent function (such as xDaysAgo) are also referentially transparent. The same rule holds true for the other functional properties: purity and totality. This helps us out a lot when we're building specialized functions out of more general ones, as we can start with confidence and keep that confidence at every step.

Now, let's take a look at another example of partial application that is both fun and shows its usefulness.

In the following example, we define a function that returns or prints the label for an envelope used to mail a letter, using the name of the recipient, the postal address, and so on. This function could be defined as follows:

```
let printEnveloppeLabel = (~firstname: string, ~lastname: string, ~address:
string, ~country: string)
  : unit => {
  print_newline();
  print_endline(firstname ++ " " ++ lastname);
```

```
        print_endline(address);
        print_endline(country);
};
```

We can call the function the normal way, with all of its parameters, as follows:

```
printEnveloppeLabel("John", "Doe", "Some address in the US", "USA");
```

We can also define another function for partial application, passing a value for the country parameter, as follows:

```
let printEnveloppeLabelUS = printEnveloppeLabel(~country="USA");
printEnveloppeLabelUS("John", "Doe", "Some address in the US");
```

We can also pass a value for the `lastname` parameter, for a function that prints the label for the members of the same household, as follows:

```
let printEnveloppeLabelDoeFamily = printEnveloppeLabelUS(~lastname="Doe",
~address="Some address in the US");
printEnveloppeLabelDoeFamily(~firstname="Jane");
```

The execution of the JS resulting from the compilation of this example (`src/Ch07/Ch07_Currying.re`) gives the following output:

```
John Doe
Some address in the US
USA

John Doe
Some address in the US
USA

Jane Doe
Some address in the US
USA
```

Functions as values

In the previous section, we covered how function definitions syntactically **desugar** (that is, slightly more cumbersome syntax is used) into a series of chained function values. Let's examine the idea that functions are actually first-class values in Reason, just as much as things like numbers, strings, records, and so on.

Function literal syntax

Reason provides strong support for so-called **function literals,** also known as **lambdas** or **closures**. This means that, as in JavaScript and various other languages, we can directly write down function values wherever it's legal to write down any value. The following is the basic syntax for a function literal:

```
PATTERN => body
```

The following is the syntax for writing a curried function:

```
PATTERN1 => PATTERN2 => ... => PATTERNn => body
```

Reason provides a familiar-looking syntactic sugar for writing a curried function, as follows:

```
(PATTERN1, PATTERN2, ..., PATTERNn) => body
```

Notice the deliberate use of PATTERN, as with bindings, as follows:

```
let PATTERN = VALUE;
```

Indeed, Reason functions (whether literal or normal function bindings) can always directly pattern match on their parameters. As with any pattern match, however, we must be cautious about matching against refutable patterns in function parameters, because those risk failing at runtime. The following snippet includes examples of function literals:

```
/* src/Ch07/Ch07_FunctionLiterals.re */
let addV1(int1, int2) = int1 + int2; /* (1) */
let addV2 = (int1, int2) => int1 + int2; /* (2) */
let addV3 = int1 => int2 => int1 + int2; /* (3) */

/** A way to convert values of type ['a] to and from floats. */
module FloatConverter = {
 /* (4) */
 type t('a) = {encodeExn: 'a => float, decodeExn: float => 'a};

 /* (5) */
 let float = {encodeExn: float => float, decodeExn: float => float};
 let int = {encodeExn: float_of_int, decodeExn: int_of_float}; /* (6) */
};

let greet = ({Ch03_Domain.Person.id, name}) => /* (7) */
 {j|Hello, $name with ID $id!|j};
```

This file shows quite a lot of things, explained as follows:

1. We define a function using the syntax we've been using throughout the book, for comparison.
2. How to define and immediately bind a function literal using the slightly desugared Reason syntax.
3. How to define and immediately bind a function literal using the fully desugared curried syntax. The important thing to realise here is that these three functions are of exactly the same type and behavior, and can be called in exactly the same way: addV*n*(1, 2).
4. How to define a type that can contain two functions: one to convert a given type, 'a, to a float, and another to convert the float back to that same 'a. Note that we use the naming convention to show that both functions can potentially throw exceptions, because we can't guarantee beforehand that every type 'a can actually be converted to and from float.
5. How to define a FloatConverter.t(float), which (trivially) knows how to convert a float to a float. The functions are implemented as simply float => float, which in this context means to return the same float that was received as input.
6. How to define a FloatConverter.t(int) that knows how to convert between int and float, using functions available in the Reason standard library for comparison.
7. Finally, we saw how to define another greeter function by creating a function literal, using destructuring pattern matching of the parameter and binding the function to the name greet.

Eta abstraction

Notice that, in the preceding sixth point, we used two standard library-provided functions directly as values. We could have wrapped them inside first-class functions instead, as follows:

```
let int = {
  encodeExn: int => float_of_int(int),
  decodeExn: float => int_of_float(float)
};
```

Wrapping something inside a function in general is called **eta abstraction**. It's an abstraction because it adds a layer of indirection instead of returning a value straight away. In other words, we first need to pass in an argument, which is substituted inside the body of the function, before the calculated result is returned.

In some cases, an eta abstraction is necessary. For example, our preceding float converter needed a way to convert a `float` to a `float` in order to fit inside the type we set up. For that purpose, the eta abstraction `float => float` is perfect. However, eta abstraction is redundant when it wraps a single function call directly, for example, `int =>` `float_of_int(int)` or `output => Js.log(output)`. This is because that single function call is already an equivalent eta abstraction; it already takes the same parameter and calculates the same result. Thanks to Reason functions being values, we can always pass them around directly.

Often, when we're concentrating on writing the functions we need, it's easy to miss these redundancies. Luckily, we can remove redundant eta abstractions when simplifying the codebase at a later date, and without changing the meaning of the code.

Summary

Functions are an important part of Reason and are used a lot. This chapter focused on presenting their essential properties: referential transparency, purity, and totality. We also discussed the specific techniques involved with Reason functions, such as currying and partial application.

In the next chapter, we are going to look at more approaches and techniques supported in Reason that help in code reuse and programming generically.

8
Reusing Code with Many Different Types

In previous chapters, we covered a lot of specific techniques. Among others, we have seen how modules are used to package code that defines types and values. We have also seen functions and function types, including their usage techniques, such as currying and partial application.

In this chapter, we are going to build on what we have seen so far, and cover the following topics:

- Polymorphism techniques in Reason
- Generic code with modules and functors

Polymorphism in Reason

Polymorphism, a category of technique used in many programming languages, allows for writing code that can apply to different types or objects (in languages such as C++ or Java, for example). Looking at things precisely shows that there are several techniques or kinds of polymorphism.

We will discuss two of those ways of doing polymorphism here:

- Parametric polymorphism
- Ad hoc polymorphism

Generic functions with parametric polymorphism

Parametric polymorphism allows a function or a data type to be written in a generic way, meaning that it can handle values in the same way regardless of their type. This is both interesting and powerful, since it implies that functions written using parametric polymorphism work on different data types.

 In C++, parametric polymorphism is usually known as **generic programming** or **compile-time polymorphism**.

We can perform parametric polymorphism with types in ReasonML. There is a special feature we use to do it, **type variables**, which we already encountered in Chapter 7, *Making Types that Represent Operations*, in one of the examples related to *function literals*. Instead of using a concrete type such as int or string for a parameter or result, we use type variable. So, using type variable as the type of a parameter would make sure that values of any type are accepted.

 A function that uses type variables is called a **generic function**.

Let's explain with an example. The *identity* function is the usual simple example that helps explain what a generic function is. The identity function (let's call it id()) just returns its input parameter. It is defined as follows:

```
let id = x => x;
```

Based on that definition, ReasonML infers the type of the input parameter using 'a, meaning it uses a type variable to indicate that values of any type are accepted. And the return type of the function is inferred in the same way, as the type of its parameter, the 'a type variable. That is the behavior of a generic function.

 Whenever we have a type name starting with ', such as 'a (meaning *any type*), this defines a type variable.

Here, is another example of such a function. We can think of a function (lastElem) that returns the last element of a list. The point is that the elements of the list could be of any type. In addition to that, since we must account for the empty list case, we will use the option type with type variable.

We can write an interface for the function (see in the src/Ch08/Ch08_GenericFunctionLastElementOfList.rei file) as follows:

```
let lastElem: list('a) => option('a);
```

And, based on how lists work in Reason, we can define a **recursive** function (using the rec keyword), as follows:

```
let rec lastElem = aList =>
  switch aList {
  | [] => None
  | [x] => Some(x)
  | [_, ...l] => lastElem(l)
};
```

Let's test it with the following Js.log calls:

```
Js.log(lastElem([1, 3, 2, 5, 4]));
Js.log(lastElem(["a", "b", "c", "d"]));
```

As expected, the output (see the src/Ch08/Ch08_GenericFunctionLastElementOfList.re file) shows 4 and d as resulting values.

Ad hoc polymorphism or overloading

Ad hoc polymorphism is the other technique we are going to discuss now. It is also known as **overloading,** and it provides different implementations for the same operation, such as the + operation. To stick with this example, we may find in some programming languages, such as Python, that the + operation has an implementation for the addition of numbers, another one for string concatenation, and a third one for list or array concatenation.

 Ad hoc polymorphism is supported by almost all programming languages for built-in operations, such as +, −, and *.

ReasonML does not currently support ad hoc polymorphism. So, for example, we have the distinct + operator for `int` addition, the +. one for float addition, and the ++ one for string concatenation. And, if needed, we have to manually convert values into the right types before applying a given operator to them.

 ReasonML may eventually support ad hoc polymorphism via the modular implicits currently being developed.

Generic code with functors

As we have seen, modules are important in OCaml and ReasonML, helping to organize code into units with specified interfaces. In addition to that, we are going to see now that they can serve for building generic code using what are called **Functors**.

What is a functor?

A functor is a function whose parameters are modules and whose result is a module.

Functors allow us to extend existing modules with new functionality, without requiring a lot of repetitive code for the different types we have.

The syntax of functors looks as follows:

```
module F = (M1: I1, ···): ResultI => {
   ...
};
```

With these characteristics, note the following:

- The F functor has as parameters one or more M1 modules and so on
- Each parameter module must be typed via an interface (I1 for M1 and so on)
- The interface for the result type (ResultI) is optional

Some examples will help us understand.

Example 1 – looking in the standard library

The best example is the `Set` module that comes with the standard library.

A `Set` type has an ordering (for example, in the set of the integer numbers, *1 < 2* and *2 > 1*), and elements are unique. Note that we have that in other languages, such as Python, too.

To use sets in ReasonML and OCaml, you first have to make one. You do that by calling `Set.Make`, which is a functor. It takes as input another module that must have a `compare()` function implemented within it and returns our `Set` type module.

We can write this, for example, for a set of integers:

```
module IntSet =
    Set.Make(
        {
            let compare = Pervasives.compare;
            type t = int;
        }
    );
```

We get a new module that provides functions for conveniently working with sets of integers, such as `IntSet.of_list()`:

```
let myIntSet = IntSet.of_list([1,2,3]);
```

Let's display the result in the console:

```
Js.log(myIntSet)
```

When we use the `node` command to run the JS file generated by compiling that program file (`src/Ch08/Ch08_FunctorsExample1.re`), we get output showing the created `IntSet`:

```
[ 0, 1, [ 0, 2, [ 0, 3, 0, 1 ], 2 ], 3 ]
```

With this first example, we got an idea of how functors work.

Example 2

Here's another example taken from the ReasonML documentation, also about sets, that we are going to discuss. We will show a `MakeSet` functor that takes in a module of the `Comparable` type and returns a new set that can contain such comparable items.

We start by defining the `Comparable` type, as follows:

```
module type Comparable = {
   type t;
   let equal: (t, t) => bool;
};
```

Now, we define the functor, as follows:

```
module MakeSet = (Item: Comparable) => {
   /* 1 */
   type backingType = list(Item.t);
   let empty = [];
   let add = (currentSet: backingType, newItem: Item.t) : backingType =>
     if (List.exists((x) => Item.equal(x, newItem), currentSet)) {
       currentSet /* 2 */
     } else {
       [
         newItem,
         ...currentSet /* 3 */
       ]
     };
};
```

Here is this code block explained:

(1) We use a list as our data structure.

(2) If the item exists, return the same set.

(3) Else, prepend to the set and return it.

Now, let's remember that we want to create a set, the items of which are pairs of integers. We create the input module, `IntPair`, which abides by the `Comparable` signature required by `MakeSet`, as follows:

```
module IntPair = {
   type t = (int, int);
   let equal = ((x1, y1), (x2, y2)) => x1 == x2 && y1 == y2;
   let create = (x, y) => (x, y);
};
```

This means that we can write the following, using the functor:

```
module SetOfIntPairs = MakeSet(IntPair);
```

To finish, let's add some code to use the resulting module:

```
let aSetOfPairItems: SetOfIntPairs.backingType = SetOfIntPairs.empty;
Js.log(aSetOfPairItems);
let otherSetOfPairItems = SetOfIntPairs.add(aSetOfPairItems, (1, 2));
Js.log(otherSetOfPairItems);
let thirdSetOfPairItems = SetOfIntPairs.add(otherSetOfPairItems, (2, 3));
Js.log(thirdSetOfPairItems);
```

This should be enough to get something interesting.

When we use the `node` command to run the JS file generated by compiling our Reason code file (`src/Ch08/Ch08_FunctorsExample2.re`), we get the following output:

```
0
[ [ 1, 2 ], 0 ]
[ [ 2, 3 ], [ [ 1, 2 ], 0 ] ]
```

What have we done? Using a functor, we were able to create a module, `SetOfIntPairs`, from another module. The new module has the `add` function, among other things. Using the module, we can create an empty set (`0` in the output), to which we can add pairs of `int` instances on demand (using the previously mentioned `add` function).

Example 3

We will now use an example from Axel Rauschmayer that can be found in his repository, at `https://github.com/rauschma/reasonml-demo-functors`.

To be precise, let's use the Printable pair functor example, with a small adaptation, to help us easily understand how this can be useful.

Before defining the functor, we must define the interface of its parameters. Here, we will have a single parameter, the `PrintablePair` module. For that, we will define a first type, `PrintableType`, that will be used by `PrintablePair`. We define it as follows:

```
module type PrintableType = {
    type t;
    let print: t => string;
};
```

Now, we add the definition of the `PrintablePair` type, as follows:

```
module type PrintablePair = (First: PrintableType, Second: PrintableType)
=> {
  type t;
  let make: (First.t, Second.t) => t;
  let print: (t) => string;
};
```

We can then define the functor, as follows:

```
module Make: PrintablePair = (First: PrintableType, Second: PrintableType)
=> {
 type t = (First.t, Second.t);
 let make = (f: First.t, s: Second.t) => (f, s);
 let print = ((f, s): t) =>
   "(" ++ First.print(f) ++ ", " ++ Second.print(s) ++ ")";
};
```

Now, we have the code where we are going to use the functor, starting with defining the `PrintableString` and `PrintableInt` modules.

We define `PrintableString` as follows:

```
module PrintableString = {
  type t=string;
  let print = (s: t) => s;
};
```

And, we define `PrintableInt` as follows:

```
module PrintableInt = {
  type t=int;
  let print = (i: t) => string_of_int(i);
};
```

Now, we add the rest of the code, as follows:

```
module PrintableSI = Make(PrintableString, PrintableInt);
let () = PrintableSI.({
  let pair = make("Jane", 53);
  let str = print(pair);
  print_string(str);
});
```

When we use the `node` command to run the generated JS code (from the Reason file, `src/Ch08/Ch08_FunctorsExample3.re`), we get the following output:

```
(Jane, 53)
```

We are done!

Summary

We have seen that ReasonML supports parametric polymorphism using `type variables`, one of the language features. When using `type variable` as the type of a function's parameter, values of any type are accepted for that parameter. This technique allows writing what we call generic functions and plays an important part in code reusability in ReasonML.

In contrast, ad hoc polymorphism, the other kind of polymorphism that is supported in popular programming languages, does not yet exist in ReasonML. But work is in progress to correct that lack in a future version.

Modules also play an important role in code reuse. But, that's not all. In addition to what they allow by themselves, ReasonML has a powerful feature that augments what we can do with them: *functors*. They are like special functions that take one or several modules as input and return a module. That opens up some possibilities in terms of programming generically.

In the next chapter, we are going to explore ReasonML techniques for extending types to add behavior.

Extending Types with New Behavior

9

In the previous chapter, we have seen that Reason provides tools and techniques that open possibilities for programming generically. One is parametric polymorphism using type variables. Another one is the functor, which can take one or several modules as parameters and return a module.

In this chapter, we are going to look at ways of extending types themselves to add behavior to them. One such technique available in Reason is called **subtyping**. The idea is to have a hierarchical relation of types, with specific types being subtypes of more generic types. For example, a *cat* could be a subtype of *mammal*, which itself is a subtype of *vertebrate*.

We can find a definition about the subtyping approach in the OCaml documentation:

> *Subtyping governs when an object with one type A can be used in an expression that expects an object of another type B. When this is true, we say that A is a subtype of B. More concretely, subtyping restricts when the coercion operator* e :> t *can be applied. This coercion works only if the type of e is a subtype of t.*

In addition to subtyping, there are techniques similar to what we do with **Object-Oriented Programming (OOP)**-style inheritance, which can be useful.

Depending on the situation and use cases, you can leverage one or several of these techniques to improve your code's structure and make it easy to extend its features, while keeping your code type-safe.

In this chapter, we will cover the following topics:

- Subtyping using polymorphic variants
- Code reuse with OOP-style inheritance

Subtyping using polymorphic variants

As we have seen in `Chapter 5`, *Putting Alternative Values in Types*, Reason has the concept of variant types, which can be leveraged in pattern matching and exhaustivity checking. Variant types have their more complex and powerful version called **polymorphic variants**. They give us more flexibility than regular variants. Among other things, they are defined using a special syntax, such as `type color = [`Red | `Orange | `Yellow | `Green | `Blue];`, and their constructors exist independently.

Let's see how they can be used for extending type behavior using subtyping.

Reusing constructors for different types

Since constructors exist independently, we can use the same constructor more than once. So, we can define a type, `rgb`, that uses the `Red`, `Green`, and `Blue` constructors that came with the definition for the type, `color`.

Here, we start with both type definitions, followed by a couple of bindings to use those types (`onegreen` and `othergreen`):

```
type color = [`Red | `Orange | `Yellow | `Green | `Blue ];
type rgb = [`Red | `Green | `Blue];

/* Bindings using the variants we defined */
let onegreen: color = `Green;
let othergreen: rgb = `Green;
```

Let's also add code to show the values:

```
/* Console log */
Js.log(onegreen);
Js.log(othergreen);
```

At this point, if you try executing the JavaScript resulting from the compilation of this Reason code, you would get output similar to this:

```
756711075
756711075
```

As we can see, the identifier printed is the same for both variables, which we could have had the intuition of, since we have used the same constructor (`Green`).

Let's make this visually interesting by adding functions that stringify the values.

We add a function that gives a string value for each color, as follows:

```
let stringOfColor = (c: color) : string => {
  switch (c) {
  | `Red => "red"
  | `Orange => "orange"
  | `Yellow => "yellow"
  | `Green => "green"
  | `Blue => "blue"
  }
};
```

We add a function that gives a string value for each *RGB color*, as follows:

```
let stringOfRgb = (c: rgb) : string => {
  switch (c) {
  | `Red => "RGB red"
  | `Green => "RGB green"
  | `Blue => "RGB blue"
  }
};
```

And we add the same code that is useful to log the values, as follows:

```
Js.log(stringOfColor(onegreen));
Js.log(stringOfRgb(othergreen));
```

So, what's the result of this new experiment? The compilation of the complete version of the code (in the `src/Ch09/Ch09_Example1.re` file) gives a JS code file which, when executed using the `node` command, would give an output similar to this:

```
756711075
756711075
green
RGB green
```

As you would have guessed, using two different functions, we were able to differentiate the output based on the type of the input (and the constructor involved, for example, the polymorphic constructor, `Green`).

As an exercise left for the reader, add `Js.log(stringOfRgb(onegreen));` to the ReasonML code and see what you get as output for that call.

An example of polymorphic variant type extension

There is a more interesting trick of code reuse. It is possible to extend an existing polymorphic variant type to create a new one. Let's see this through another example.

Let's say we want to handle input for shoe categories, for both the general public and for women, and we started by defining the categories specific to women, as follows:

```
type onlyWomanShoe = [`Slingbacks | `HighHeels];
```

We could define the polymorphic variants for all (women and men) by reusing that type definition and extending it, as follows:

```
type shoe = [onlyWomanShoe | `Moccasins | `Boots | `Sneakers | `Wingtips];
```

We can see the result of these types with the code file, `src/Ch09/Ch09_Example2.re`. As usual, we add some console logging (with `Js.log()`) to make things interesting. The complete code is as follows:

```
type onlyWomanShoe = [`Slingbacks | `HighHeels];
type shoe = [onlyWomanShoe | `Moccasins | `Boots | `Sneakers | `Wingtips];

let johndoe_shoe: shoe = `Moccasins;
let janedoe_shoe: shoe = `Slingbacks;

Js.log(johndoe_shoe);
Js.log(janedoe_shoe);

let infoAboutShoe = (s: shoe) : string => {
 switch (s) {
 | `Slingbacks => "Slingbacks – Specific woman shoe"
 | `HighHeels => "High Heels – Specific woman shoe"
 | `Moccasins => "Moccasins"
 | `Boots => "Boots"
 | `Sneakers => "Sneakers"
 | `Wingtips => "Wingtips"
 }
};

Js.log(infoAboutShoe(johndoe_shoe));
Js.log(infoAboutShoe(janedoe_shoe));
```

Executing the JS code that results from the compilation gives an output similar to the following:

```
265261402
-594895036
Moccasins
Slingbacks - Specific woman shoe
```

It is interesting to see what could happen at compile time if you make a mistake when binding the constructor to the `janedoe_shoe` variable, for example, writing the following:

```
let janedoe_shoe: onlyWomanShoe = `Slingbacks;
```

Try it, and during re-compilation, you will immediately see an error similar to the following:

```
This has type:
  onlyWomanShoe
But somewhere wanted:
  shoe
The first variant type does not allow tag(s)
`Boots, `Moccasins, `Sneakers, `Wingtips
```

Now, back to our normal code! Could we improve our code here to write less? Could we leverage the variants type, `onlyWomanShoe`, in the `infoAboutShoe()` function, to avoid the two lines in the `switch` block for `Slingbacks` and `HighHeels`, and try to make this really powerful?

There is a trick to do that, using a syntax sugar within the `switch` block of the function: `#onlyWomanShoe`.

We will explain in detail later where this comes from, but basically we could write this almost-equivalent code (`src/Ch09/Ch09_Example2bis.re`), where we only change the body of the `infoAboutShoe` function, as follows:

```
let infoAboutShoe = (s: shoe) : string => {
    switch (s) {
        | #onlyWomanShoe => "Woman shoe such as Sandals or High Heels"
        | `Moccasins => "Moccasins"
        | `Boots => "Boots"
        | `Sneakers => "Sneakers"
        | `Wingtips => "Wingtips"
    }
};
```

Executing the JS code produced by the compilation gives output such as the following:

```
265261402
-594895036
Moccasins
Woman shoe such as Slingbacks or High Heels
```

More about extending polymorphic variant types

Suppose we have a type definition for websites and we want to extend it to all web apps (including personal productivity tools, social networks, and even APIs). We could first define the main things that characterize a website, such as the following:

- The domain
- Whether there is an access by login or not (for the main content), that is, private or public access

To get started, we can first define two utility types, `domain` and `accessType`, as follows:

```
type domain = [ `Domain(string) ];
type accessType = [`Private | `Public];
```

Then, we add a helper function to stringify the `accessType` values:

```
let accessTypeName = (a: accessType) : string => {
switch (a) {
| `Private => "private"
| `Public => "public"
}
};
```

Now, let's define the variants type for websites:

```
type website = [
| `CorporateSite(domain)
| `CommerceSite(domain, accessType)
| `Blog(domain, accessType)
];
```

We then add a function that would return a short summary text containing the information for each website:

```
let siteSummary = (app: website) : string => {
 switch (app) {
 | `CorporateSite(`Domain(s)) => s ++ " - corporate site (public)"
 | `CommerceSite(`Domain(s), a) => s ++ " - commerce site (" ++
accessTypeName(a) ++ ")"
 | `Blog(`Domain(s), a) => {
 switch (a) {
 | `Private => s ++ " - " ++ "corporate blog (" ++ accessTypeName(a) ++ ")"
 | `Public => s ++ " - blog (public - login-based access for authors)"
 }
 }
 }
};
```

As usual, for testing purposes, we add a few bindings and show the results in the console using Js.log():

```
let mysite = `CorporateSite(`Domain("www.acme.com"))
Js.log(siteSummary(mysite))

let myblog = `Blog(`Domain("www.contentgardening.com"), `Public)
Js.log(siteSummary(myblog))

let corpinternalblog = `Blog(`Domain("internalblog.acme.com"), `Private)
Js.log(siteSummary(corpinternalblog))
```

We can see that part working. But, we are not done yet. We also want to extend that code to apply to any webapp. So, we define a new type, for *web apps* (webapp, as you would guess) with the intent of being an extension of the *websites* one. The type definition is as follows:

```
type webapp = [
 | `CorporateSite(domain)
 | `CommerceSite(domain, accessType)
 | `Blog(domain, accessType)
 | `SocialApp(domain)
];
```

After that, we add a new function (appSummary()) that will extend the previous one (siteSummary()). One technique we use here is the as keyword, allowing us (in the switch part of the function) to match a result to a constructor of the website variant type. For example, we can write `CorporateSite(`Domain(s)) as ws.

We can define the function as follows:

```
let appSummary = (app: webapp) : string => {
  switch (app) {
  | `CorporateSite(`Domain(s)) as ws => siteSummary(ws)
  | `CommerceSite(`Domain(s), a) as ws => siteSummary(ws)
  | `Blog(`Domain(s), a) as ws => siteSummary(ws)
  | `SocialApp(`Domain(s)) => s ++ " - social app"
  }
};
```

Note that we can actually improve this a little bit; to avoid the compiler from complaining about the s and a variables not being used in the first three lines of the switch block, we can replace those variables by the _. The improved function is as follows:

```
/* 1) the extended function **/
let appSummary = (app: webapp) : string => {
  switch (app) {
  | `CorporateSite(`Domain(_)) as ws => siteSummary(ws)
  | `CommerceSite(`Domain(_), _) as ws => siteSummary(ws)
  | `Blog(`Domain(_), _) as ws => siteSummary(ws)
  | `SocialApp(`Domain(s)) => s ++ " - social app"
  }
};
```

We can finish by adding some testing code, as follows:

```
Js.log("---")
let fb = `SocialApp(`Domain("facebook.com"))
Js.log(appSummary(fb))
```

But wait, there is more improvement possible!

Another technique is to reuse the first type via the #website as ws syntax and that allows us to completely replace the lines related to the website variant type constructors in the pattern matching.

The final version of the function would then be as follows:

```
/* 2) the extended function improved! **/
let appSummaryImproved = (app: webapp) : string => {
  switch (app) {
  | #website as ws => siteSummary(ws)
  | `SocialApp(`Domain(s)) => s ++ " - social app"
  }
};
```

And, after this update, to make things interesting, here is the final testing and value display code:

```
Js.log("------")
Js.log(appSummaryImproved(mysite))
Js.log(appSummaryImproved(myblog))
Js.log(appSummaryImproved(corpinternalblog))
Js.log(appSummaryImproved(fb))
```

We can see that executing the JavaScript code produced by the compilation gives the following output:

```
www.acme.com - corporate site (public)
www.contentgardening.com - blog (public - login-based access for authors)
internalblog.acme.com - corporate blog (private)
---
facebook.com - social app
------
www.acme.com - corporate site (public)
www.contentgardening.com - blog (public - login-based access for authors)
internalblog.acme.com - corporate blog (private)
facebook.com - social app
```

We just saw a nice type extension technique supported by Reason with polymorphic type variants.

Code reuse with OOP-style inheritance

Inheritance, as we have in object oriented programing languages, is not commonly used in Reason. However, we can find a couple of examples of techniques that resemble OOP-style inheritance.

Opening a module

Constantly referring to something in a module imposes a lot of writing on the developer. This is where open is handy.

Without this feature, let's say you have the ColorExample module (based on code we already used in the first example of this chapter), defined as follows:

```
/* A module */
module ColorExample = {
    type color = [`Red | `Orange | `Yellow | `Green | `Blue ];
```

```reason
type rgb = [`Red | `Green | `Blue];

let onegreen: color = `Green;
let othergreen: rgb = `Green;

let stringOfColor = (c: color) : string => {
  switch (c) {
      | `Red => "red"
      | `Orange => "orange"
      | `Yellow => "yellow"
      | `Green => "green"
      | `Blue => "blue"
  }
};

let stringOfRgb = (c: rgb) : string => {
  switch (c) {
      | `Red => "RGB red"
      | `Green => "RGB green"
      | `Blue => "RGB blue"
  }
};
}
```

You can use the function by using the `ColorExample.stringOfColor` reference and similarly for the values. So, some value display code would look like the following (as actually seen in the `src/Ch09/Ch09_Open_module.re` file):

```reason
/* Use the module the default way */
Js.log("1/ Use function and values inside the module...");
Js.log(ColorExample.stringOfColor(ColorExample.onegreen));
Js.log(ColorExample.stringOfRgb(ColorExample.othergreen));
```

But, with the `open` solution for opening the module within a scope, we can write more compact code, as follows (in the same `src/Ch09/Ch09_Open_module.re` file):

```reason
/* Open the module and use its content */
Js.log("2/ Use function and values from the module after opening it...");
let colorString = {
  open ColorExample;
  let oneblue: color = `Blue;
  Js.log("String value of another color: " ++ stringOfColor(oneblue));
};
```

And things work as expected! The code file when executed gives the following output:

```
1/ Use function and values inside the module...
green
RGB green
2/ Use function and values from the module after opening it...
String value of another color: blue
```

What happens is that all of the contents of the module are magically accessible without the need to add the prefix that would normally be added (the `ColorExample.` part, in this case) when accessing the types, functions, and variables it contains. It brings the module's content into the current scope.

We could have done things in an alternative way: have the module in its own file for better separation of code. There are cases where you would want to do that if it better fits your way of organizing the code. So basically, let's move the module's code in the `src/Ch09/Ch09_OpenModulebisPart1.re` file, for example, as follows:

```
module ColorExample = {
  type color = [`Red | `Orange | `Yellow | `Green | `Blue ];
  type rgb = [`Red | `Green | `Blue];

  let onegreen: color = `Green;
  let othergreen: rgb = `Green;

  let stringOfColor = (c: color) : string => {
    switch (c) {
        | `Red => "red"
        | `Orange => "orange"
        | `Yellow => "yellow"
        | `Green => "green"
        | `Blue => "blue"
    }
  };

  let stringOfRgb = (c: rgb) : string => {
    switch (c) {
        | `Red => "RGB red"
        | `Green => "RGB green"
        | `Blue => "RGB blue"
    }
  };
}
```

Then, in another code file (`src/Ch09/Ch09_OpenModulebisPart2.re`, for example), we can open the module and access its functions and values, as follows:

```
open Ch09_OpenModulebisPart1.ColorExample;

Js.log(stringOfColor(onegreen));
Js.log(stringOfRgb(othergreen));

let colorString = {
  let oneblue: color = `Blue;
  Js.log("String value of another color: " ++ stringOfColor(oneblue));
};
```

That's it! We have seen how to leverage `open` for opening modules in Reason. And, in code that you can find written by other developers, you can find it used a lot.

Including a module

Reason also provides a way to reuse a module already defined, and extend it like in OOP: the `include` keyword.

Regarding this feature, the documentation actually says the following:

> Using `include` *in a module, statically transfers a module's content into a new one. Thus often fulfills the role of inheritance or mixing.*

Let's say we have a base module as follows:

```
module Site = {
  let siteEnvMarker = "TESTING";
  let protocol = (~secured) => secured ? "https" : "http";
  let getInfo = domainName => protocol(~secured=false) ++ "://" ++
  domainName ++ " (" ++ siteEnvMarker ++ ")";
};
```

Now, we reuse it in the following module, using the `include` technique, as follows:

```
module ProductionSite = {
  include Site;
  let siteEnvMarker = "production!";
  let getPublicInfo = domainName => {
  let additionalText = " (" ++ String.uppercase(siteEnvMarker) ++ ")";
  let result = protocol(~secured=true) ++ "://" ++ domainName ++
additionalText;
  Js.log(result);
  }
};
```

And, we can display information using a function from each module, in order to compare the behavior:

```
Js.log(Site.getInfo("dev-acme.com"));
print_newline();
ProductionSite.getPublicInfo("acme.com");
```

Executing the JS code produced by compiling our code (in the `src/Ch09/Ch09_Include_module.re` file) gives the following output:

```
http://dev-acme.com (TESTING)

https://acme.com (PRODUCTION!)
```

Interesting. You could already have the intuition of what happens here, but the ReasonML documentation about `include` stipulates that this technique copies over the definition of a module *statically*, then also performs `open`.

Summary

We have now seen how you can leverage two types of techniques, subtyping using polymorphic variants and OOP-style inheritance with modules, to improve your code structure and make it easy to add behavior to types.

With polymorphic variant types, we can reuse constructors for different types because of their design. Furthermore, it is possible to extend a polymorphic variant type to create a new one.

With modules, we can open an existing module to use functions and bindings defined in it, and we can include it in a new module to extend its behavior line in OOP-style inheritance.

In the next and last chapter, we are going to go through a final example where we bring together the main techniques we have learned so far.

10
Bringing It All Together

In the previous chapters, we explored the different tools and techniques available for doing type-driven development in ReasonML.

In this chapter, using a final example, we are going to develop a sense for when to use each type-driven technique to solve problems. Let's see how we could, at least partly, create code that handles input (within a small JavaScript app) for social, productivity, and business applications. To be precise, what we mean here are the kinds of successful applications, such as Gmail, Facebook, Twitter, Skype, Airbnb, or Uber, launched by Internet or platform companies.

In this chapter, we will cover the following topics:

- Starting with a variant type (version 1)
- Using more pattern matching (version 2)
- Switching to polymorphic variant types (version 3)
- Using records (version 4)
- Using modules for code structure (version 5)
- An alternative code structure (version 6)
- An improvement: Using lists as output (version 7)
- Another improvement: Using mutable records (version 8)
- Unit testing our code (final version)

Starting with a variant type (version 1)

First, we need a `type` to represent the companies, which are internet-powered apps. Based on that `type`, we can think of writing functions that will help us build our logic in a type-safe manner. Let's see how it goes.

As a first attempt, we start small, defining a variant type for the internet companies we are interested in. As we have seen in previous chapters, we will use pattern matching to show the list of apps each of these companies delivers to their users.

We define the internet company type as follows:

```
type internetCompany =
  | Facebook
  | Google
  | Twitter;
```

Now, we define the function that shows the applications, based on the company, as follows:

```
let apps = (company: internetCompany) : string => {
  switch (company) {
    | Facebook => "facebook, messenger, ads"
    | Google => "gmail, google+, maps, ads"
    | Twitter => "twitter"
  }
};
```

The following code will show some apps from Google:

```
let googleApps = apps(Google);
Js.log(googleApps);
```

Here is the output of the whole code (generated from `src/Ch10/Ch10_PlatformCompany_V1.re`):

```
gmail, google+, maps, ads
```

That's a good start.

Since there are different categories of applications involved (social, business, communication, entertainment, and so on), we could enrich our type-driven logic by using more pattern matching code to differentiate the list of applications. Let's do that now.

Using more pattern matching (version 2)

If we change the variants' constructors to pass a string to them to represent each possible category (for example `Facebook(string)`, which could give `Facebook("social")` or `Facebook("business")`), we can do the trick. The additional pattern matching could then be something like this:

```
Facebook(str) => switch str {
        | "social" => "facebook, messenger, instagram"
        | "business" => "facebook ads"
```

So, let's start the second version of our code by defining the internet company variant type, as follows:

```
type internetCompany =
    | Facebook(string)
    | Google(string)
    | Twitter(string);
```

And, as we planned, our function's pattern matching code could evolve, as follows:

```
let apps = (company: internetCompany) : string => {
  switch (company) {
    | Facebook(str) => switch str {
        | "social" => "facebook, messenger, instagram"
        | "business" => "facebook ads"
    }
    | Google(str) => switch str {
        | "social" => "google+, gmail"
        | "business" => "google ads, google adsense, gmail for business"
    }
    | Twitter(str) => switch str {
        | "social" => "twitter"
        | "business" => "twitter ads"
    }
  }
};
```

Now, the following code will show some result data, so we can see whether things work as expected:

```
Js.log(Js.String.toUpperCase("facebook"))
Js.log("Business: " ++ apps(Facebook("business")));
Js.log("Social: " ++ apps(Facebook("social")));

Js.log(Js.String.toUpperCase("google"))
Js.log("Business: " ++ apps(Google("business")));
Js.log("Social: " ++ apps(Google("social")));
```

Here is the output we get when executing this version (`src/Ch10/Ch10_PlatformCompany_V2.bs.js`, generated from `src/Ch10/Ch10_PlatformCompany_V2.re`):

```
FACEBOOK
Business: facebook ads
Social: facebook, messenger, instagram
GOOGLE
Business: google ads, google adsense, gmail for business
Social: google+, gmail
```

Note that our type only accounts for internet companies, but our logic should also apply to other modern companies that use technology (web mobile, databases, AI) to build and deliver services in a scalable way. We can call them **platform companies**. So, we could add a type for platform companies too.

We can even consider that some internet companies (the big ones at least) are also platform companies or have launched platform businesses. So, we could change from *normal variant types* to *polymorphic variant types* to use their capability for type reuse.

Let's start the third version based on these new ideas.

Switching to polymorphic variant types (version 3)

In this new version, we define the two types we build our logic around, reusing the first one inside the second one, as follows:

```
type internetCompany = [ `Facebook(string) | `Google(string) |
`Twitter(string) ];
type platformCompany = [ internetCompany | `Amazon(string) | `Uber(string)
]
```

Based on that, we make our function evolve as follows (using platformCompany to allow all the variants to be accepted for the company parameter):

```
let apps = (company: platformCompany) : string => {
  switch (company) {
    | `Facebook(str) => switch str {
      | "social" => "facebook, messenger, instagram"
      | "business" => "facebook ads"
    }
    | `Google(str) => switch str {
      | "social" => "google+, gmail"
      | "business" => "google ads, google adsense, gmail for business"
    }
    | `Twitter(str) => switch str {
      | "social" => "twitter"
      | "business" => "twitter ads"
    }
    | `Amazon(str) => switch str {
      | "social" => ""
      | "business" => "amazon, AWS"
    }
    | `Uber(str) => switch str {
      | "social" => ""
      | "business" => "uber"
    }
  }
};
```

And now, let's add the usual quick data display code, as follows:

```
Js.log(Js.String.toUpperCase("facebook"))
Js.log("Business: " ++ apps(`Facebook("business")));
Js.log("Social: " ++ apps(`Facebook("social")));
Js.log("")

Js.log(Js.String.toUpperCase("google"))
Js.log("Business: " ++ apps(`Google("business")));
Js.log("Social: " ++ apps(`Google("social")));
Js.log("")

Js.log(Js.String.toUpperCase("uber"))
Js.log("Business: " ++ apps(`Uber("business")));
```

That seems like a good improvement, but let's see whether it works. Testing the generated JavaScript code (based on `src/Ch10/Ch10_PlatformCompany_V3.re`) gives the following output:

```
FACEBOOK
Business: facebook ads
Social: facebook, messenger, instagram

GOOGLE
Business: google ads, google adsense, gmail for business
Social: google+, gmail

UBER
Business: uber
```

Nice! What could we add to that?

Although this implementation is nice, you can quickly see it lacks the ability to handle a richer data structure. Basically, we would like to represent an *app* with all the needed information, such as *the name*, and *the URL* (at least for web apps). For that, Reason has a convenient tool we can use: *records*.

Let's see how it goes with the next version, using records to handle apps.

Using records (version 4)

Nothing changes from our first variant types, but we will add the `webapp` record type definition to them, as follows:

```
type internetCompany = [ `Facebook(string) | `Google(string) |
`Twitter(string) ];
type platformCompany = [ internetCompany | `Amazon(string) | `Uber(string)
];
type webapp = {
  name: string,
  url: string,
};
```

Then, we can input some data for the rest of the program, using that record type, as follows:

```
/* some data */
let facebook: webapp = {
  name: "facebook",
  url: "https://facebook.com",
```

```
}
let facebookads: webapp = {
  name: "facebook ads",
  url: "https://www.facebook.com/business",
}
let messenger: webapp = {
  name: "messenger",
  url: "https://www.facebook.com/messenger",
}
let instagram: webapp = {
  name: "instagram",
  url: "https://www.instagram.com",
}
```

Note that we just defined a few of those values for a minimal test. The real production-ready code should include all the record values needed.

The minimal `apps` function would then look like the following:

```
let apps = (company: platformCompany) : string => {
  switch (company) {
    | `Facebook(str) => switch str {
        | "social" => facebook.name ++ ", " ++ messenger.name ++ ", " ++
instagram.name
        | "business" => facebookads.name
      }
  }
};
```

Let's add some output display code, as follows:

```
Js.log(Js.String.toUpperCase("facebook"));
Js.log("Business: " ++ apps(`Facebook("business")));
Js.log("Social: " ++ apps(`Facebook("social")));
```

We get the following output for that minimal testing case (code from the `src/Ch10/Ch10_PlatformCompany_V4.re` file):

```
FACEBOOK
Business: facebook ads
Social: facebook, messenger, instagram
```

In the next version, we will also use the URL of each app and show it in the output.

We can also improve the global code structure by packaging some types and functions in modules.

Using modules for code structure (version 5)

The first improvement we can make is to create a module to contain the record for the web apps and a function that would return their string representation. Let's call that module `WebApp`. Its definition is as follows:

```
module WebApp = {
  type t = {
    name: string,
    url: string,
  };

  let toString = (app: t) => app.name ++ " (" ++ app.url ++ ")" ;
}
```

Then, as in the previous version, we have our example web app values. The only thing that changes is that the type annotation is done using `WebApp.t`. That part of the code is as follows:

```
let facebook: WebApp.t = {
  name: "facebook",
  url: "https://facebook.com",
}
let facebookads: WebApp.t = {
  name: "facebook ads",
  url: "https://www.facebook.com/business",
}
let messenger: WebApp.t = {
  name: "messenger",
  url: "https://www.facebook.com/messenger",
}
let instagram: WebApp.t = {
  name: "instagram",
  url: "https://www.instagram.com",
}
```

We then create a module, called `Platform`, for the rest of the logic. It could contain the definition of the types for companies and the `apps` function. To make things simple, let's choose to have a unique polymorphic variant type that contains all the companies. Within the module, we can call it `t`.

We create the module as follows:

```
module Platform = {
  type t = [ `Facebook(string)
           | `Google(string)
           | `Twitter(string)
           | `Amazon(string)
           | `Uber(string)
           ];

  let apps = (company: t) : string => {
    switch (company) {
      | `Facebook(str) => switch str {
         | "social" => WebApp.toString(facebook) ++ ", " ++
WebApp.toString(messenger) ++ ", " ++ WebApp.toString(instagram)
         | "business" => WebApp.toString(facebookads)
      }
    }
  };
}
```

We can add a similar code that shows some possible output, and the code execution (JS code generated from the `src/Ch10/Ch10_PlatformCompany_V5.re` file) gives us an output similar to this:

```
FACEBOOK
Business: facebook ads (https://www.facebook.com/business)
Social: facebook (https://facebook.com), messenger
(https://www.facebook.com/messenger), instagram (https://www.instagram.com)
```

Our result is encouraging. There may be different possibilities, so let's continue experimenting by trying an alternative code structure and later adding improvements.

An alternative code structure (version 6)

At this point, it's actually possible to write comprehensive code while using fewer modules in our code file. Let's keep the platform module, but move out what we had in the `WebApp` module in *Using modules for code structure (version 5)*, thus eliminating that module. At the same time, we will adjust some names and definitions.

While we have fewer modules, we can improve our type-based code by introducing an interface file (src/Ch10/Ch10_PlatformCompany_V6.rei) to hold type information for the .re file (src/Ch10/Ch10_PlatformCompany_V6.re), as follows:

```
type webapp;
type pfcompany;

let appToString: webapp => string;
```

Next, we define the webapp and pfcompany types and adjust the appToString function accordingly (in src/Ch10/Ch10_PlatformCompany_V6.re), as follows:

```
/* Basic types and functions we need (see .rei file) */

type webapp = {
    name: string,
    url: string,
};

type pfcompany = [ `Facebook(string)
                 | `Google(string)
                 | `Twitter(string)
                 | `Amazon(string)
                 | `Uber(string)
                 ];

let appToString = (app: webapp) => app.name ++ " (" ++ app.url ++ ")" ;
```

Then, there is no algorithmic change in the part where we do the *let bindings* to have input data for the web apps, so because of readability, we will not repeat that part of the code here. You can see the complete set of record values in the src/Ch10/Ch10_PlatformCompany_V6.re file, and you will notice that we added input for some Google apps, as shown here:

```
/* Data */

/* ...
   Extract from src/Ch10/Ch10_PlatformCompany_V6.re */

let google: webapp = {
  name: "google",
  url: "https://google.com",
}
let gmail: webapp = {
  name: "gmail",
  url: "https://google.com/gmail",
}
```

```
let googleads: webapp = {
  name: "google ads",
  url: "https://ads.google.com",
}
let googleplus: webapp = {
  name: "google+",
  url: "https://plus.google.com",
}
```

Next, we improve the Platform module code:

- We have the Platform module, which is preceded by its signature, PlatformType.
- We're using pfcompany now as the type for the company values.
- We added the case of Google (and their apps) in the code for pattern matching in the apps function.

The improvised part of the platform module code is as follows:

```
/* Platform module, signature followed by implementation */

module type PlatformType = {
  let apps: pfcompany => string;
};

module Platform: PlatformType = {
  let apps = (company: pfcompany) : string => {
    switch (company) {
      | `Facebook(str) => switch str {
          | "social" => appToString(facebook) ++ ", " ++
appToString(messenger) ++ ", " ++ appToString(instagram)
          | "business" => appToString(facebookads)
      }

      | `Google(str) => switch str {
          | "social" => appToString(googleplus)
          | "business" => appToString(googleads)
      }
    }
  };
}
```

To make this version of the implementation easily testable, we add the usual input and output printing code, as follows:

```
Js.log("Facebook")
Js.log("Business: " ++ Platform.apps(`Facebook("business")));
Js.log("Social: " ++ Platform.apps(`Facebook("social")));
print_newline();
Js.log("Google")
Js.log("Business: " ++ Platform.apps(`Google("business")));
Js.log("Social: " ++ Platform.apps(`Google("social")));
```

To recap, we improved the type declarations using a .rei file (which helps with code documentation), we added a module signature (PlatformType) for platform, and we improved the coverage of the input by adding the Google case.

The reader is encouraged to add input data (for the other companies in the variant type, such as Twitter, Amazon, and Uber).

An improvement – using lists as output (version 7)

You noticed that in our output, we are just using strings (via concatenation). From the beginning, we could have returned a real list of the apps from each company. No problem, let's change the code to do that now.

The change is limited to the Platform module. In the signature, for the apps function, we change the output type from string to list(string). And, in the pattern matching part of the function, we change the implementation accordingly, for example, by returning the [appToString(facebook), appToString(messenger), appToString(instagram)] list for Facebook apps.

The main part of the new version is as follows:

```
/* Platform module, signature followed by implementation */

module type PlatformType = {
  let apps: pfcompany => list(string);
};

module Platform: PlatformType = {
  let apps = (company: pfcompany) : list(string) => {
    switch (company) {
      | `Facebook(str) => switch str {
```

```
            | "social" => [appToString(facebook), appToString(messenger),
appToString(instagram)]
            | "business" => [appToString(facebookads),]
        }

      | `Google(str) => switch str {
          | "social" => [appToString(googleplus),]
          | "business" => [appToString(googleads),]
      }
    }
  };
}
```

Since we now output lists, it is a good idea to use `Array.of_list` to print them, since it is a nice and quick solution. We change the last part of the code with the following:

```
Js.log("Facebook")
print_string("Business: ")
Js.log(Array.of_list(Platform.apps(`Facebook("business"))));
print_string("Social: ")
Js.log(Array.of_list(Platform.apps(`Facebook("social"))));
print_newline();

Js.log("Google")
print_string("Business: ")
Js.log(Array.of_list(Platform.apps(`Google("business"))));
print_string("Social: ")
Js.log(Array.of_list(Platform.apps(`Google("social"))));
```

Executing the resulting code with my input data gives the following output:

```
Facebook
Business: [ 'facebook ads (https://www.facebook.com/business)' ]
Social: [ 'facebook (https://facebook.com)',
  'messenger (https://www.facebook.com/messenger)',
  'instagram (https://www.instagram.com)' ]

Google
Business: [ 'google ads (https://ads.google.com)' ]
Social: [ 'google+ (https://plus.google.com)' ]
```

Nice! This was an interesting improvement. Let's continue adding to it.

Another improvement – using mutable records (version 8)

Now, we could use a mutable record for the webapp type, so that we use it for interesting app data that keeps updating. One such data point is the number of accounts created. Another one could be the number of downloads of the corresponding mobile app.

In this example, let's see how we can improve our implementation by adding the *number of accounts* parameter to the record. This is done by using mutable numberOfAccounts: int as the entry for that parameter in the record definition.

So that's the only change for now, but let's recap the definitions for the webapp type, the pfcompany type, and the appToString function for better readability, as follows:

```
type webapp = {
    name: string,
    url: string,
    mutable numberOfAccounts: int,
};

type pfcompany = [ `Facebook(string)
                 | `Google(string)
                 | `Twitter(string)
                 | `Amazon(string)
                 | `Uber(string)
                 ];

let appToString = (app: webapp) => app.name ++ " (" ++ app.url ++ ")" ;
```

After that, let's add a function that increments the value of numberofAccounts in the record corresponding to a web app each time there is a new sign-up. This function could look as follows:

```
let newSignUp = (app: webapp) : unit => {
  app.numberOfAccounts = app.numberOfAccounts + 1;
  ()
};
```

Then, as before, we have the input data part. But now we have the new parameter `newSignUp` which we have to keep updating. To make things simple, let's pretend that all these apps currently have the same number of accounts, and we choose 10,000 as an arbitrary number. So, now the record definitions are as follows:

```
/* Data */

let facebook: webapp = {
  name: "facebook",
  url: "https://facebook.com",
  numberOfAccounts: 10000,
}
let facebookads: webapp = {
  name: "facebook ads",
  url: "https://www.facebook.com/business",
  numberOfAccounts: 10000,
}
let messenger: webapp = {
  name: "messenger",
  url: "https://www.facebook.com/messenger",
  numberOfAccounts: 10000,
}
let instagram: webapp = {
  name: "instagram",
  url: "https://www.instagram.com",
  numberOfAccounts: 10000,
}
let google: webapp = {
  name: "google",
  url: "https://google.com",
  numberOfAccounts: 10000,
}
let gmail: webapp = {
  name: "gmail",
  url: "https://google.com/gmail",
  numberOfAccounts: 10000,
}
let googleads: webapp = {
  name: "google ads",
  url: "https://ads.google.com",
  numberOfAccounts: 10000,
}
let googleplus: webapp = {
  name: "google+",
  url: "https://plus.google.com",
  numberOfAccounts: 10000,
}
```

There is no change in the `Platform` module part, so let's move to the next and last part, the code that tests things:

```
Js.log("Facebook")
print_string("Business: ")
Js.log(Array.of_list(Platform.apps(`Facebook("business"))));
print_string("Social: ")
Js.log(Array.of_list(Platform.apps(`Facebook("social"))));
print_newline();

Js.log("New sign-up on Instagram")
newSignUp(instagram);
Js.log("New sign-up on Instagram")
newSignUp(instagram);
Js.log(instagram.numberOfAccounts)
```

Executing the code compiled from the `src/Ch10/Ch10_PlatformCompany_V5.re` file gives the following output:

```
Facebook
Business: [ 'facebook ads (https://www.facebook.com/business)' ]
Social: [ 'facebook (https://facebook.com)',
  'messenger (https://www.facebook.com/messenger)',
  'instagram (https://www.instagram.com)' ]

New sign-up on Instagram
New sign-up on Instagram
10002
```

So, we just took an interesting use case where mutable records can be used, and saw how easy it is to add that functionality.

Unit testing our code (final version)

Now is the time to add tests to our code! For a complete demonstration, let's create a new package in which we will do the necessary setup for writing unit tests with the `Jest` framework.

Another web technology used at Facebook, `Jest` is a framework for writing tests for JavaScript code, which also works with compile-to-JavaScript languages, such as TypeScript or ReasonML. For Reason, we also need to install the `bs-jest` package, which provides bindings for Jest in BuckleScript.

Creating our final package and setting up for tests

To quickly get things working, we create a folder, called `Ch10-final`, which contains the following file structure:

```
bsconfig.json
package.json
src
__tests__
```

We got the `package.json` file by copying the one we were using, generated by the ReasonML or BuckleScript code starter, and adapting it. The first version is as follows:

```
{
  "name": "Ch10-final",
  "version": "0.1.0",
  "scripts": {
    "build": "bsb -make-world",
    "start": "bsb -make-world -w",
    "clean": "bsb -clean-world"
  },
  "keywords": [
    "BuckleScript"
  ],
  "author": "",
  "license": "MIT",
  "devDependencies": {
    "bs-platform": "^4.0.7",
  },
  "dependencies": {}
}
```

Then, we can add `Jest` and `bs-jest` (the one referenced by `glennsl/bs-jest`, to be precise) as development dependencies to our package using `npm`.

To install `bs-jest`, run the `npm install @glennsl/bs-jest --save-dev` command.

To install `Jest`, run the `npm install jest --save-dev` command.

With these installations, the required files are installed in the usual `node_modules` subdirectory and our `package.json` file changes to reference both dependencies with the versions that were installed. The updated `devDependencies` in the `package.json` file shows the two additions, as seen in the following extract:

```
"devDependencies": {
    "@glennsl/bs-jest": "^0.4.5",
    "bs-platform": "^4.0.7",
    "jest": "^23.6.0"
},
```

The `bsconfig.json` file is also copied (and adapted) from the one we were using for the previous code setup (which allows the `bsb -w` command to work, and our `.re` files to be compiled on the fly). We adjust the `sources` list to reference both the `src` directory for the usual code and the `__tests__` directory for the *test code* (notice the `"type": "dev"` part), as follows:

```
"sources": [
    {
        "dir" : "src",
    },
    {
        "dir": "__tests__",
        "type": "dev",
    },
],
```

The last thing we need to add is the `@glennsl/bs-jest` reference to the `bs-dev-dependencies` parameter. We will see why in a minute.

The `bsconfig.json` file for our `ch10final` package is as follows:

```
{
    "name": "ch10final",
    "version": "0.1.0",
    "sources": [
        {
            "dir" : "src",
        },
        {
            "dir": "__tests__",
            "type": "dev",
        },
    ],
    "package-specs": {
        "module": "commonjs",
```

```
      "in-source": true
    },
    "suffix": ".bs.js",
    "bs-dependencies": [
    ],
    "bs-dev-dependencies": ["@glennsl/bs-jest"],
    "warnings": {
      "error" : "+101"
    },
    "namespace": true,
    "refmt": 3
}
```

In the `src` subdirectory, we can add our final Reason code file (`src/Ch10-final/src/Ch10_PlatformCompany.re`). Our ReasonML code is exactly the same as in the previous version (the `src/Ch10/Ch10_PlatformCompany_V8.re` file), except that we simplify it by removing the last bit (the snippet that prints some output).

Now, let's write the tests.

Writing our first tests

To test code using `Jest`, we must start by opening the module:

```
open Jest;
```

Then, we define a `describe` function to encapsulate the tests suite. We need to open the `Expect` module, part of `Jest`, which provides the `expect` function with other things where we need to check that some values meet certain conditions. We also open the module file, which contains our implementation code. So far, our test function contains the following:

```
describe("Platform", () => {
  open Expect;
  open Ch10_PlatformCompany;

});
```

Now, we can add a first test to verify the data returned by the `apps` function in the `Platform` module. The test suite code is as follows:

```
describe("Platform", () => {
  open Expect;
  open Ch10_PlatformCompany;

  test("list facebook business app", () => {
    let facebook_biz = Platform.apps(`Facebook("business"));
    expect(facebook_biz) |> toEqual([ "facebook ads
(https://www.facebook.com/business)" ]);
  });
});
```

Let's not stop here and add a second test that verifies that the number of accounts is the previous number incremented by 1 after the `newSignUp` function has been called.

The complete tests suite code is as follows (in the `src\Ch10-final\__tests__\Platform_test.re` file):

```
open Jest;

describe("Platform", () => {
  open Expect;
  open Ch10_PlatformCompany;

  test("list facebook business app", () => {
    let facebook_biz = Platform.apps(`Facebook("business"));
    expect(facebook_biz) |> toEqual([ "facebook ads
(https://www.facebook.com/business)" ]);
  });
  test("instagram number of accounts", () => {
    let nb = instagram.numberOfAccounts;
    newSignUp(instagram);
    expect(instagram.numberOfAccounts) |> toEqual(nb + 1);
  });
});
```

Running the tests

Before we can execute the tests, we need to build the code using the `bsb -make-world` command. This finds the test code and compiles it. If everything goes well, that process copies the resulting files in the `lib` part (generated) of the package structure (under `src\Ch10-final\lib\bs\__tests__`). We are now ready to run the tests.

To run the tests, we use the `Jest` command. In my case, running this on Windows, the executable is actually located at `node_modules\.bin\jest`, but in your case, you could just type `jest`.

When we execute the `Jest` test runner command, we get the following output:

```
PASS  __tests__/Platform_test.bs.js
  Platform
    √ list facebook business app (16ms)
    √ instagram number of accounts (2ms)

Test Suites: 1 passed, 1 total
Tests:       2 passed, 2 total
Snapshots:   0 total
Time:        8.433s
Ran all test suites.
```

At this point, we have a good structure, including a test suite, and we can build on it. We can extend the input part of the code to take all the *platform companies* into account and add more functionalities. And we can add more tests as we go. This is left as an exercise for the reader.

Summary

In this chapter, we built some type-safe code that is also relatively easy to maintain and extend, using Reason's core features. We could go further to have more generic code using advanced techniques, such as functors, but that is not necessary for this small example.

This was the final chapter. We iterated through a type-driven process of solving coding problems. While doing so, we improved our understanding of ReasonML's features and techniques, in particular variant types, functions, modules, and records. We also looked at how to test ReasonML code directly using the `Jest` framework.

I hope the book was useful as an introduction to the world of ML languages, and that it will help you go further with the ReasonML techniques and tools, and maybe even with React if you are a web developer with additional skills.

Other Books You May Enjoy

If you enjoyed this book, you may be interested in these other books by Packt:

Learn WebAssembly
Mike Rourke

ISBN: 9781788997379

- Learn how WebAssembly came to be and its associated elements (text format, module, and JavaScript API)
- Create, load, and debug a WebAssembly module (editor and compiler/toolchain)
- Build a high-performance application using C and WebAssembly
- Extend WebAssembly's feature set using Emscripten by porting a game written in C++
- Explore upcoming features of WebAssembly, Node.js integration, and alternative compilation methods

Learn React with TypeScript 3
Carl Rippon

ISBN: 9781789610253

- Gain a first-hand experience of TypeScript and its productivity features
- Transpile your TypeScript code into JavaScript for it to run in a browser
- Learn relevant advanced types in TypeScript for creating strongly typed and reusable components.
- Create stateful function-based components that handle lifecycle events using hooks
- Get to know what GraphQL is and how to work with it by executing basic queries to get familiar with the syntax
- Become confident in getting good unit testing coverage on your components using Jest

Leave a review - let other readers know what you think

Please share your thoughts on this book with others by leaving a review on the site that you bought it from. If you purchased the book from Amazon, please leave us an honest review on this book's Amazon page. This is vital so that other potential readers can see and use your unbiased opinion to make purchasing decisions, we can understand what our customers think about our products, and our authors can see your feedback on the title that they have worked with Packt to create. It will only take a few minutes of your time, but is valuable to other potential customers, our authors, and Packt. Thank you!

Index

G

generalized algebraic data types (GADTs) 80
generic code
  with functors 118
generic function
  about 116
  with parametric polymorphism 116, 117
generic programming 116
generic types 85, 86, 87

H

hidden errors
  code, analyzing for 8
Hindley-Milner (H-M) type inference 86

I

implementation files 29
inheritance 60
interfaces 33
interpolation 87

J

JavaScript objects
  types 61, 62

L

lambdas 112
list
  about 88, 89, 90
  using, as output 150

M

module errors
  about 36
  signature mismatch 36, 38
module signatures
  about 33
  public API, documenting 34
  public API, exporting 34
  syntactic module signatures 35
module types 35
modules
  about 29

using, for code structure 146, 147
mutable parameterized types
  about 92
  array 92
  array of values, managing 94, 95
  ref 92
  reference, managing to value 92, 93, 94
  restrictions 97, 98, 99
mutable record fields 52, 53
mutable records
  using 152, 153, 154

N

namespaces 29
node package manager (npm) 11

O

object-oriented programming (OOP) 59, 125
observable effects 105
OCaml Package Manager (OPAM) 11
OCaml
  reference 9
OOP-style inheritance
  code, reusing 133
  module, including 136, 137
  module, opening 133, 135, 136
option 90, 92
overloading 117, 118

P

partially applied function 110
pattern 69
pattern matching
  about 67
  using 141, 142
phantom types
  about 99
  difference, forcing 99, 101
pipe-forward 100
platform companies 142
polymorphic variant type extension
  example 128, 129, 130
  website, defining 130, 131, 132
polymorphic variant types
  about 75, 126

www.ingramcontent.com/pod-product-compliance
Lightning Source LLC
Chambersburg PA
CBHW060111090326
40690CB00064B/5087